Working
from the
Heart

A practical guide to loving
what you do for a living

Liz Simpson

VERMILION
LONDON

1 3 5 7 9 10 8 6 4 2

Text copyright © Liz Simpson 1999
Exercise 'What is important to you?' on page 18; Questionnaire 'Are you ready to
embrace change?' on pages 74–6; Exercise: 'Your future goals' on pages 103–5; and
Exercise 'Seeing yourself as others see you' pages 158–9 are
all copyright © Nicholson McBride 1999.

First published in the United Kingdom in 1999 by Vermilion
an imprint of Ebury Press
Random House
20 Vauxhall Bridge Road
London SW1V 2SA

Random House Australia Pty Limited
20 Alfred Street, Milsons Point,
Sydney, New South Wales 2061, Australia

Random House New Zealand Limited
18 Poland Road, Glenfield,
Auckland 10, New Zealand

Random House South Africa (Pty) Limited
Endulini, 5A Jubilee Road,
Parktown 2193, South Africa

Random House UK Limited Reg. No. 954009

A CIP catalogue record for this book is available from the British Library

ISBN 0 09 181958 X

Designed and edited by Margot Richardson
Proofread by Kathie Gill · Index by Ingrid Lock
Printed and bound in Great Britain by
Biddles Book Manufacturers

Papers used by Vermilion are natural, recyclable products made from wood grown
in sustainable forests.

Contents

Acknowledgements   5
Foreword   7

Introduction   9

Chapter one
Taking a new attitude to work   20

Chapter two
Will the real YOU please stand up?   44

Chapter three
How much do you willingly embrace change?   70

Chapter four
What do you really want to do?   97

Chapter five
Do you work purely for the money?   116

Chapter six
Why isn't your working life more fun?   134

Chapter seven
Are your working relationships making you unhappy?   147

Chapter eight
Are your work and the rest of your life in balance?   168

Chapter nine
Working at 'Being'   180

HeartWork™   186
Further Reading   187
Index   189

To Paul

You know why

Acknowledgements

There is little a modern-day commentator can write about that age-old philosophers haven't said long before, therefore I see myself as an agent, not a source of the ideas presented in this book. My intention is to put a unique spin – based on my own life experience and perspective – on principles that have stood the test of time. In that sense, I feel rather like a Hollywood director who takes a classic film and re-packages it for a new audience.

I am indebted to the wisdom of the many long-dead poets, philosophers and spiritual teachers whose work has coloured my thinking and inspired me to make radical changes in my own attitudes to life, and work in particular. Also to the following (very much alive) individuals who have generously shared their wisdom and experience on the universal challenge we face to become happier, more fulfilled individuals in all areas of our lives.

Special thanks to business psychologists Rob Yeung, Rachel Fisher and Ruth Colling of the London office of Nicholson McBride, who kindly devised the questionnaires, quizzes and self-help exercises on pages 18, 74–6, 103–5 and 158–9, which remain their copyrighted material. I am indebted to their generosity and enthusiasm as well as their professional expertise.

Thanks also to Larry Hochman, former director of people and culture at Air Miles; Mark Hunt of Allied Domecq; Simon Woodroffe of Yo!Sushi; the Institute of Personnel and Development; Rowena Davies and her colleagues at British Airways' Careerlink; Professor Cary Cooper of UMIST; personal coach Eileen Mulligan; plus Jackie Sinden, Peter Harvey and Martine Delamere for their help with case histories. To international change agent Paul Kitson of Paul Kitson Associates for generously sharing his knowledge, particularly of some of the exercises in Chapter Six, 'Why isn't your working life more fun?', which he has successfully used with organisations around the world. Similarly, to Piers Ibbotson, a freelance director with the Royal Shakespeare Company.

Other vital contributions came from Nella Barkley, president of the Crystal-Barkley Corporation in New York; Robert Holden of the Happiness Project; my friends at Time/system; spiritual author Marianne Williamson; Chris McAndie; and James Grimster of Orangeleaf for designing the HeartWork™ website.

Last, but certainly not least, I would like to extend my grateful thanks to all the wonderful editors – including Fiona MacIntyre at Random House, Sandra Harris at *Business Life* magazine and Pepi Sappal at *Human Resources* magazine – for helping to make my working life so fulfilling and enjoyable. And to all the people I admire who consistently prove that you can be successful in business and still remain a warm and wonderful human being.

Liz Simpson

Foreword

This book can be approached on various different levels. From a purely pragmatic standpoint it can help you take a more positive attitude to the changing world of work, and it suggests ways to enhance your employability. It can help you uncover the kind of work you feel passionate about so that, when you wake up most mornings, you know there is nothing else you would rather do with your working hours; in short, it will help you find the fit between your values, interests and abilities. But it also has a deeper purpose, which may make greater sense if I begin by sharing with you my philosophy of life: how I make sense of who I am, and what I'm doing here.

As a Buddhist, I view life as a virtual-reality commando course for spiritual warriors learning to be human beings. I believe that before we take on a new incarnation we choose what advantages and disadvantages we are going to test ourselves against in terms of gender, race, parents or caregivers, social background, financial standing: the entire backdrop of our human lives. The purpose of the game – through the way we face and overcome the challenges presented to us – is to recover, and then hone and refine our souls. With each Herculean hardship and Odyssean challenge we are given the opportunity to collect 'soul credits', which I imagine to be like shards of light that, fitted together, shine like a diamond within us to fill the world with love and joy. Those individuals who endure and, hopefully, transcend the greatest pain and challenges in life are undoubtedly the most courageous spirits of all.

Spirits who complete the game successfully don't need to re-take the course and so become one with God, while those who haven't scored the necessary credits when 'game over' is signalled by death, return in another lifetime for another try. There is no sense of failure in this, just another wonderful opportunity to experience the emotions we cannot feel in spirit form.

I believe fervently that, through the work we do – paid or unpaid, from accountancy to saving the whales – we can find much to help us rediscover and purify our souls, including authenticity, integrity, devotion, service, fulfilment and passion.

That is why, should you choose to do so, you can look beyond this book's advice on how simply to become more employable and successful at work, and start to regard the expression of your gifts as an essential training ground for your spiritual 'passing out' ceremony.

Introduction

"Each of us was created to give outward expression to Divinity through our personal gifts. Sharing our gifts with the world is our Great Work, no matter what our job description might be or how our résumé reads."
Sarah Ban Breathnach

Anita Roddick admits she didn't know anything about business when she opened the first Body Shop in England in 1976. In a recent interview, Simon Woodroffe, the managing director of the spectacularly successful Yo!Sushi in London, told me he knew nothing about restaurants when he launched his business in January 1997. Similarly, Isaac Tigrett, who co-founded the Hard Rock Cafe back in the 1960s, had no experience in that industry either. There are many other, less well-known individuals who have achieved great success – however you choose to interpret that word – without academic qualifications or traditionally accepted skills, simply by choosing to put their heart into their work.

I know: I'm one of them. Although I had no background in television presenting or journalism when I launched my media career twelve years ago, this was the work I felt I had been born to do. In fact, all the early signs were there that journalism was my vocation or 'calling', but I allowed myself to become slightly sidetracked along the way. Until I became a journalist and author I hated my work.

As a child, I dreamed of being either a television producer or a journalist. I always had my head in one book or another, day-dreamed constantly, loved amateur dramatics and produced short stories and makeshift magazines in which I wrote all the material. I was in the school debating team, which honed my presentation skills, and one year wrote, produced and starred in (the latter only because the leading lady and understudy were both sick at the last minute) a play based on the Egyptian mythical tale of Osiris.

However, at the age of 21, having spent an unhappy three years since school working at the BBC in various secretarial capacities (they turned me down as a potential producer!), I decided a media career was obviously not for me and drifted into temping before taking on various permanent positions, first as a secretary then as a marketing executive, in very hierarchical organisations. This only led to more frustration until, despairing of ever finding a fulfilling job, destiny took a hand. I became pregnant with my first child and, somewhat relieved to be out of the rat race, eased myself into the role of homemaker and mother.

I had given up on my dream at the first hurdle because I had never considered what was the right environment for me to work in, not just the right job. And because I kept my focus on what I *didn't* want to do for a living, that's exactly what I got. Yet life always wants to support us and, like Thomas Edison's numerous attempts to produce a light bulb that worked, I gradually came to realise that each of these 'failures' was skilling me up and offering valuable self-understanding with which to draw closer to the work I now love.

"Several years ago I reached a proverbial career crossroads. It was then that I discovered the key ingredient in any decision-making process: passion. If you let passion inform your decisions, you'll make good ones."
**Anne Sweeney, President,
The Disney Channel, California**

When we consider what to do for a living, most of us are so fixated on the *what* and the *how* that we rarely ask ourselves why we want to follow a particular line of work. Rarely do we think about the type of environment that would suit us best, or the kind of people we would like to work with. It was only when I recognised that I have all the attributes of self-motivation, self-confidence, a love of variety and the freedom to work flexibly that I realised I am a miserable employee but ideally suited to freelance work. I am not a team player (I detested team games at school: another clue!) and because I like to generate and work on my own ideas, working with other people on a day-to-day basis frankly isn't my cup of tea. The jobs I had before my career break were well paid, my colleagues were nice, friendly, helpful people, but the truth was *my heart wasn't in what I was doing*. The work just wasn't 'me'. Today it's a very different story. I wake up every morning fired up with enthusiasm because there is nothing else I want to do for a living than write, run workshops, talk on TV or radio shows or speak at some event or other. Let me explain how that came about.

Somewhat bored at home with two youngsters under the age of five, and having taken voluntary work on various local community projects as far as I felt they could go, I began writing on an old typewriter on the dining-room table. First, short stories that appeared regularly in a Scottish newspaper, and then my first book, which was accepted – and remained largely unedited – by the first publisher I sent it to. Things really took off from there and involved a series of 'synchronicitous' events – which is what happens when you start working from the heart – that led me to becoming a television presenter, then a freelance journalist, psychology student, editor of a personal development magazine, consultant editor of a new mind, body and spirit magazine, author, conference speaker and workshop facilitator.

Like Anita Roddick, Simon Woodroffe and Isaac Tigrett, I might not have had the 'proper' qualifications many people consider are necessary before embarking on a particular venture, but I had a passion and talent for communication in many of its forms. I was not only good at writing but opportunities presented themselves to me constantly. People who work from the heart find that, while life still offers them daily challenges, there is an ease with which their talents are expressed in the job they do. They are not just happy in their work, but successful too.

Anita Roddick may not have known about the ins and outs of business, but she was a consumer who passionately wanted something different to what was being offered at that time in the beauty industry, and believed in herself enough to provide it. I don't need to remind you how amazingly successful The Body Shop has been in the past twenty-odd years.

Simon Woodroffe, previously a designer of stage sets for the likes of Queen, Elton John and Rod Stewart, fuels his new business with the same creativity that brought him success working on rock shows. He doesn't just think about how to offer his customers great food, great service and very good prices, but how they can have a party every night. He brings to his new role as restaurateur a passion for producing the spectacular experience, and has taken that company from a standing start to a turnover of £2 million in the first year.

Isaac Tigrett helped build a world-famous business on gut instinct and love and is quoted as saying: 'There simply weren't any guidelines for creating the kind of place I had in my mind and heart.' At its foundation, the Hard Rock Cafe instituted respectful, loving principles towards its staff and customers, including the first profit-sharing plan in any restaurant in England, incentivised on the basis of friendliness, helpfulness and being part of a 'family'. Plus, he paid his female employees exactly the same as males at a time when this was unheard of (which still includes today!). He knew, in his heart, what he wanted from a restaurant experience then worked towards providing that for his customers. Essentially, Isaac Tigrett made a fortune out of believing that – in the famous words of The Beatles – 'All you need is love'.

'Are you your job?' is a question occupational psychologists frequently ask nowadays, concerned that many people's self-esteem and security are tied into what they do for a living. That's a valid concern. However, I believe it is time to ask a new question: 'Is your job you?' What we need to learn to do is how to be skilful at listening to our hearts as well as our heads when it comes to our work, and become familiar with the excitement of waking up each day knowing there is nothing else we would rather do with the time devoted to earning a living. Look at it this way: working 40 hours a week, for 48 weeks of the year for an average of 40 years equates to 76,800 working hours in a lifetime. That's a long time in which to be unhappy.

> *"A soulful approach to work is probably the only way an individual can respond creatively to the high temperature stress of modern work life without burning to a crisp in the heat."*
> **David Whyte, The Heart Aroused**

Passion and work; to many of us they seem completely contradictory. Indeed, when I spoke to a group of inner-city college leavers about setting their sights on work that they felt passionate about, rather than taking the first dead-end job offered to them, there was a lot of embarrassed laughter: because passion is something we more commonly associated with relationships and sex. The tragedy is, many people's working lives become like their marriages where passion has been exchanged for comfort, security and predictability. Very safe, yes, very boring, certainly, and for many of us likely to precipitate a living death. In an uncertain world, while it is tempting to cling on to what we know, it can be incredibly life-enhancing to let go of the cliff face to which we are painfully hanging for dear life and trust that we will paraglide safely to whatever destination life will lead us: and passion is the fuel that can help us do that.

It has never been a more important time for organisations to embrace people who are driven by passion rather than pure pragmatics in their work. One leading commentator on emotional capital (the concept that capturing employees' hearts more than their minds is becoming crucial to an organisation's success, and should therefore be quantified as an asset on its balance sheet) found that while challenge, stress and commitment are current emotional drivers, what will propel the most innovative and hence successful companies in the future is the passion of its people. Why? Because the major reason customers take their business elsewhere, and never return, is indifferent or discourteous service. Now think about how you behave when doing a job your heart isn't in. Do you exhibit the sort of attitude that attracts or repels others in this situation? Unless you are an actor worthy of an Oscar nomination, I'd like to bet it's the latter.

Many of the world's greatest and enduring spiritual and philosophical traditions, from individuals such as Aristotle, Confucius and Buddha to profound works such as the Bible, Koran and *Bhagavadgita*, have recognised that vocational choice plays a vital role in a person's general health and happiness. One has only to look at the rising levels of sickness absence in companies to get a feel for the general malaise within the current world of employment. My experience certainly bears this out as I have never been healthier or happier since setting out on my current path. Yet I used to regularly take time off with minor complaints as a frustrated and unhappy employee.

It took me a long time to experience passion for my work, partly because I had fallen into the trap of separating myself into different categories: thinking it was normal to be a totally different person at work to the one I was at home or with close friends. It isn't. Perhaps you've experienced something like this yourself when you've worked with someone for a while and then meet them in a social situation where they seem to have undergone a personality change. Yet the key to finding that 'daily worship' at work, which spiritual teachers tell us is what we should be seeking, is to integrate who you truly are – not the social mask we each tend to construct for ourselves – with what you do for a living.

However your own career has panned out, whether you are working your way towards a particular goal or have no idea what your heart's work is, each of us is here to complete a mission: to discover the work we are born to do and in accomplishing it, find joy. By putting your unique gifts to their most appropriate use you will find work that is personally fulfilling and, if you choose to, make a positive contribution to other people's lives. That is what this book is going to help you do. Everyone can find their true vocation or 'calling' in life, whether that involves working on a factory production line or being the CEO of a major corporation; whether as a nurse or an insurance consultant; whether heeding childhood compulsions or enduring lengthy periods of unemployment.

Working from the Heart is not so much about self-development, which implies there is something about you that needs to be improved; it is a book about self-understanding, one that will help you authentically rediscover your self in order to benefit from the momentous changes that are currently taking place in the world of work. This doesn't involve changing you into someone else: it's about finding out who you really are so you can select your work to suit the real you.

None of us should underestimate how threatening it can be to look inside ourselves, which is why so many people avoid it for as long as possible, until confronted with what is commonly called the 'mid-life crisis', money problems, redundancy, or a serious illness, and are forced to do so. Few of us relish the idea of stripping our existence bare until we are faced with our spiritual nakedness. Yet it is this challenge that takes us forward, that causes us to grow into authentic human beings and, ultimately, bring us the happiness we seek.

After setting the scene for the new world of work in Chapter One, each subsequent chapter covers a particular obstacle to fulfilment at work. The first four chapters build on helping you unearth the kind of work that represents your whole self, particularly what your heart longs for, while the second four chapters deal with the challenges that often make it harder to seek out, maintain or enjoy otherwise fulfilling work. Each of these road maps includes a range of exercises to help you gain a greater understanding of yourself and how your unique life purpose can be expressed through your work, and concludes with a consolidating message in Chapter Nine.

I urge you to write down your answers to these exercises rather than just going through them in your head. Putting your thoughts on paper is an immensely powerful thing to do, as is illustrated by the story of 'The 4 per centers' (see page 16). By writing your thoughts down you can more clearly see the links you are looking for, and hence are better equipped to find the answers to your own questions.

While a lot of self-help books simply state the measures you need to take to successfully move your life forward, I want to offer you, wherever possible, explanations of why these techniques are successful. Some of these explanations come from science, particularly quantum physics; others from age-old spiritual principles. All you need to do is keep an open mind.

Well, perhaps not all: now for the bad news. Nothing in this book will help you unless or until you act on it. If you want to learn to ride a bicycle you wouldn't expect to do so just by reading about it or having someone else tell you about their experience. You would need to get on one yourself, fall off a few times and find the courage to keep jumping back on the saddle. It is only when you have achieved the skills required through experience that such knowledge stays with you for life.

The same is true of this book. Just reading it will give you an appreciation of what's involved, like reading any 'how to' book. But you will get far more out of it and experience the benefits for yourself if you commit to setting aside some quiet time, alone, to reflect on what it is you want, to engage consistently in the exercises and decide that from today you are going to do things differently. As someone once said: 'If you do what you've always done you will get what you've always got.'

By introducing you to new categories of thinking I hope you will be inspired to regard your work in a very different, life-enhancing way; to notice things about yourself you never have before; and, in fitting the two together, to achieve a job that is as joyous and fulfilling for you as mine is for me.

~ The 4 per centers ~

In 1953, Yale University carried out a piece of research among its final-year students, who were all interviewed about their opinions on the facilities, staff and courses, as well as about life in general. One of the questions the students were asked was, 'Do you have goals?' Of those interviewed, 10 per cent said, yes they did. This isn't extraordinary in itself, nor was the fact that only 4 per cent of this number said they wrote those goals down. However, in 1973, when the University was about to repeat the exercise with contemporary students, someone decided it might be a good idea to try to find the graduates who had left 20 years earlier and compare notes. Although this proved to be a demanding task, the majority of those students were tracked down and their questionnaires compared not only with those of their 1973 counterparts, but also with what they said about their lives back in the 1950s.

What the university discovered from this fascinating piece of research was that the 4 per cent of students who had written their goals down were more successful – and not just in material terms – than the others, and from a financial point of view were worth more than the combined resources of the other 96 per cent.

In his book *Mindstore*, leading UK personal development guru Jack Black describes these 4 per centers as sailors on the ocean of life who, in order to navigate life's rough seas, know that they must have a rudder and an engine to get to where they want to go. The value of writing your goals down is that it keeps your 'life boat' in the direction you have chosen, rather than allowing yourself to drift aimlessly like the 96 per cent less successful Yale graduates. It's rather like the joke of the tourist who asks an Irishman the way to Dublin and is told: 'If that's where you're going then I wouldn't start from here.' While no one can exactly predict the future, at least knowing which direction you ought to be facing is half the battle in finding the path to the work you love.

～ You are important ～

Working from the Heart deals with employment in its broadest sense. It is not a business book. Chapter One sets the scene by putting the current world of work into context but it is not my purpose to address how organisations can meet the challenges that face them. My focus is on one individual: you. What you will find peppered throughout the book, however, are case histories and business analogies to illustrate the points being made. After all, while it may be of some use to talk about fun at work theoretically, it's much more valuable to read about what others are doing so you can follow their example if you choose to.

It may not be traditional to put an exercise into one's Introduction, but since this is a book that also promotes 'out-of-the-box thinking' (see page 78), I think this is the ideal place to offer you a taste of what lies ahead, both in terms of an initial activity and how your answers will link in with the chapters that follow.

✒️ Exercise: What is important to you?

Look at the following list of personal needs, things that are important to you as an individual. They may be things you want, but
don't necessarily have, at the moment and – because we are
looking at your life as a whole right now – include both your
home environment and work.

    Now re-write this list in order of importance, with your
most highly valued need at the top. If any of the following is not a
priority for you, just leave it out. Remember, this is your list and
you don't have to show it to anyone, so you owe it to yourself to
be completely honest.

- Being appreciated for what you do
- A quiet workplace
- Flexible working hours
- Professional growth and learning
- A feeling of being involved
- Family
- Reputation
- Leisure activities
- Opportunities for promotion
- House, property and possessions
- Socialising with co-workers
- Friends
- Job security
- High salary/benefits
- Support/loyalty of your manager/boss
- Influence and power
- Getting feedback on your performance.

Keep your list safe because you will need to refer to it as you
work your way through the rest of the book. These personal
needs relate to, and are expanded upon in Chapters Two to Eight.

Now let's start by looking at the changing world of work and the opportunities it offers for sharing each of our unique gifts. As you read through the following eight chapters, bear in mind the words of Goethe:

'Whatever you can do or dream you can begin it.
Boldness has genius, magic and power in it.
Begin it now.'

---

*"The majority work to make a living;
some work to acquire wealth or fame,
while a few work because there is something within
them which demands expression."
Edmond Boreaux Szekely*

CHAPTER ONE

Taking a new attitude to work

"I've dreamt in my life dreams that have stayed with me ever after and changed my ideas.
They've gone through and through me, like wine through water,
and altered the colour of my mind."
Emily Brontë

~ Why do we work? ~

The answer to this question depends largely on the culture in which one is asking. In today's society work is linked to a variety of reasons, including:

- A structure to our lives
- Varied, enforced activity
- Social contact
- Job satisfaction
- A sense of importance
- Financial security
- Avoidance of relationship and other issues
- Status
- Certainty
- A sense of belonging.

Not surprisingly, there is huge significance attached to having a job in Western cultures – particularly paid employment – as it is the key driver behind most people's public identity and self-esteem. Just think how quickly in a conversation people ask: 'What do you do?' to which we invariably reply, 'I am a journalist, an architect, a car mechanic' or whatever. It is because we take our jobs and construct a whole identity around them that unemployment is such a psychologically distressing experience for many. It's as if we have lost a sense of who we are as well as the monthly pay packet.

This is why the first part of this book is strongly focused on helping you excavate who you really are, in terms of your values, your deepest interests and your philosophy on life. It doesn't just concentrate on the skills and experience you may have acquired over the years. I *do* journalism (among other things) but this is not the sum total of who I *am*, which makes it easier for me to shed that image when it is no longer congruent with my changing needs, enabling me to embrace a new one.

Having a 'false identity' based on what we do for a living presents an even greater challenge to our spirits in their desire for expression, when we become locked into careers because of circumstantial constraints rather than because of what our hearts want. The standard of schooling, the availability of books and other resources, parental support, the quality of career advice, ease of access to a wide choice of occupations and suchlike have all conspired to side-track us into occupational choices that don't even come close to answering our deeper needs. We then get stuck on a treadmill of justifying that enforced 'choice' because we have invested so much time in it, accruing in the process attributes or characteristics conventionally regarded as suitable for the job we do. When this happens you have to ask yourself some tough questions, including: 'If I knew my life were to end tomorrow, would I die feeling fulfilled as an individual?'

Work is a self-fulfilling prophecy. If you choose it to be about self-expression, and make the necessary commitment to uncover the work you love and feel passionate about, then your working environment, as if by a miracle, supports you. This is because when you have a compelling goal or vision, you set in motion internal and external energies that re-pattern your life. You come across as 'different' to people because you are using new vocabulary, body language and behaviours that are consistent with what you are seeing. This subconsciously magnetises you so that other people and serendipitous opportunities are drawn to help.

However, as psychological studies have found, those who consider work to be inherently stressful, boring and unfulfilling, and don't expect it to be otherwise, fail to find the motivation to improve their lot and consequently find themselves

in a situation where they loathe their work. Life always conspires with us, without judgement about what is 'right' or
'fair', to produce an environment that supports our beliefs.

~ Free yourself ~

Now is the time to free yourself from the situational and psychological constraints that may have shackled you to a job
you hate, something you do simply to fill the time before you
have earned enough money to go out and enjoy yourself. You
are now being asked to free yourself from just thinking in
terms of a career. What you will be doing throughout this
book is to seek out your vocation. This is a word that comes
from the Latin *vocare*: to call. Freeing yourself involves dis-
covering your mission, your unique purpose, whatever it is
that will make a difference to you and your impact on the
world. But the call is like a whisper in the cacophony of life.
You first have to believe it is there and then be still and quiet
enough, through periods of silent contemplation and
meditation, to hear its voice.

Incidentally, the word career comes from the French word
carrière, meaning a racecourse. Fill that racecourse with rats
and what have you got but a rat race!

This book is simply about answering two questions:

1 If you were asked to construct the perfect job for you, what
   would it be like? and
2 What are you most passionate about?

Find the link between the two and you will have found a
way to love what you do for a living. This doesn't mean an
occupation that you merely like, or one that offers you the
most money, status or any of the other 'mind-driven' criteria
we think will make us happy, but the sort of work that
really fires you up.

Here are some of the symptoms experienced when you work
from the heart, not just from the head:

● You are constantly excited and motivated by the
  challenges of your work
● You wake up looking forward to weekdays, not just
  Saturdays and Sundays

- You have more energy
- There is no other way of earning a living that you desire more
- Earning money becomes less important but you find it comes to you anyway
- You regard work-related problems as challenges that you can cope with, not insurmountable difficulties
- You begin to think in terms of what your contribution to the world of work offers others
- You are the same person inside work as you are outside
- You know that you will always find an outlet for your talents
- Your life has a purpose
- You are happy.

How many of these apply to you right now? If it is not that many, then ask yourself why you continue to accept a working situation that is less fulfilling than you desire it to be. Or, if you are currently unemployed, think about all the jobs you have taken on in the past and hated. Why shouldn't you go to work every day feeling overjoyed, enthusiastic and believing your life has a purpose? To believe that you are not only making a difference, having fun and feeling satisfied – but getting well paid into the bargain? Perhaps you don't view work in that light. If so, you are not alone. Whenever I ask the question 'What do you really want to do?' to people who have intimated that they get no pleasure from their work, I'm met with a series of common responses, such as:

- I haven't a clue. I'm too busy trying to earn a living to think about it
- It's out of my control: life is easier if you don't make waves
- You're lucky to have any job nowadays, so what's the point indulging in fantasies?
- I'm not bothered about my job, as long as I earn enough to enjoy myself at weekends
- Given the choice I wouldn't want to work at all; that's what I really wish for.

Such attitudes to work are socially constructed: that is, we learned them from society in general, from our parents, teachers, friends and colleagues. As you will shortly discover – and there's now scientific validation for this – you create your world, not the other way round. But for the moment let's take each of the above replies in turn and find out what they tell us about the way in which our society currently regards work.

I haven't a clue. I'm too busy trying to earn a living to think about it.
In our 'quick fix' western societies we're used to immediate gratification. We experience pain and, instead of taking the time to listen to what our body is telling us, we pop a pill to make it go away. Given the choice of accepting a lower paid position with the chance of greater rewards in the longer term, many people opt for an immediately higher paid job with less prospect of future advancement, their rationale being that tomorrow can take care of itself.

Western cultures are notoriously short term in their thinking, which affects many aspects of our lives, from the way governments handle the economy and organisations formulate their management strategies, to the way we view romantic relationships. In contrast, Eastern societies take a long-term, future-oriented perspective, and treat their elderly as revered, wise teachers rather than useless burdens. It is much more commonplace in Eastern cultures for individuals to practise meditation and commit themselves to a journey of self-knowledge because it is impossible to accurately know what you want and satisfy yourself vocationally until you know who you are.

Many of us spend a large part of our lives focusing on short-term material and emotional survival at the expense of our longer-term needs. Yet, if we are not going to constantly live our lives 'fire-fighting', we need to allocate some time to assessing what it is we really want out of life. Part of the reason we avoid this is because of our poverty consciousness. The prevailing notion in the Western world is that life is tough and there isn't enough of anything, particularly money and jobs, for everyone. We are therefore encouraged to become as competitive and independent as we can, which culminated in the 'me first' attitude of the 1980s. People who take the view that life happens to them rather than offering them the chance to control or shape their destiny have attitudes such as:

It's out of my control: life is easier if you don't make waves, and You're lucky to have any job nowadays, so what's the point indulging in fantasies?
These beliefs are leftovers from the days when organised religion sold us the promise of riches in heaven in exchange for accepting limitations in this life. It could be said that this is nothing more than propaganda designed to keep the masses under control and ensure power remained in the hands of an élite minority. As with all things, there is an alternative viewpoint. Instead of perpetuating the belief that sinners will be held accountable for every misdemeanour in life, the Koran, the sacred book of Islam, and the Jewish Talmud teach that at the day of reckoning, we will each be asked to answer why we refused to acknowledge life's many pleasures. Experiencing joy, rather than pain and suffering, is the purpose of life according to these religions. Many spiritually inspiring individuals down the ages, from Buddha to Deepak Chopra, have consistently broadcast the message that the moment we change the way we think to an attitude of abundance, we start to manifest our deepest desires. However, while many of us in the West no longer believe that we have to wait for riches in heaven, we are still left with the notion that life is tough.

It is true that there are fewer jobs around nowadays and many, such as those in heavy industry, have disappeared forever. It has been suggested that 50 to 60 per cent of jobs that sit between a company and its customers will disappear, replaced by 'electronic commerce'. The titles of books such as *The End of Work: The Decline of the Global Labour Force* and *The Dawn of the Post-Market Era* and *Jobshift: How to Prosper in a Marketplace without Jobs* describe the situation in a nutshell. However, the whole notion of what you believe a job to be needs to change to fit in with today's adaptable working environment. There will always be work for those adaptable and flexible enough to seize new opportunities; it's just unlikely to be with one company. In fact, it's been estimated that most of us will have five or six different employers

– if not careers – during our working lives. A year-long study by US company McKinsey & Co, involving 77 companies and nearly 6,000 business executives, revealed that talent will be the most important – and rare – corporate resource in the next 20 years. Smart, flexible, creative, self-motivated, responsible 'ideas' people who can deliver winning strategies for business will be pursued aggressively by major corporations. And, because the talent pool is predicted to be getting smaller, these people will be paid handsomely and showered with company benefits in order to stay with such corporations.

I'm not bothered about my job, as long as I earn enough to enjoy myself at weekends, and
Given the choice I wouldn't want to work at all; that's what I really wish for
If you have found yourself making statements like these in the past, then you have bought into the commonly held belief that work is synonymous with 'labour', 'toil', 'drudgery', 'chore' and 'a duty'. Many of us share this negative view of what has been described as a 'Monday through Friday sort of dying', living for the weekends when we can enjoy ourselves and dreaming of the day when we will win the lottery and can give up work for good. Yet work as a separate activity to the rest of your life is a relatively recent concept.

In Christian societies, work has been regarded as a way of avoiding idleness and hence the temptations of the flesh. This unhelpful association was developed during the Reformation, at which time work was considered to be a moral duty which could help save your soul from eternal damnation. The French writer and philosopher Voltaire captured the prevailing mood perfectly when he wrote: 'Work banishes those three great evils: boredom, vice and poverty.' However, it wasn't long before work itself was regarded as a 'great evil'. By the time Karl Marx began writing in the mid-19th century, work had been given a wholly negative interpretation, one in which workers were exploited by a capitalist society that prevented them from realising their creative potential. Is it surprising, then, that we have largely grown up with less than inspiring beliefs around the meaning of employment? Consider this assessment by contemporary social anthropologist Studs Terkel from his 1972 book *Working*:

'Work is by its very nature about violence – to the spirit as well as to the body. It is about ulcers as well as accidents, about shouting matches as well as fist-fights, about nervous breakdowns as well as kicking the dog around. It is, above all, about daily humiliations. To survive the day is triumph enough for the walking wounded among the great many of us.'

But work isn't a 'thing', it's a collection of individuals who choose to act like this – or not, as the case may be. The good news is that whatever you have learned you can unlearn. When you choose to change your thoughts and the way you interpret 'work', your outside world automatically changes to reflect your new beliefs. And we sorely need to unshackle ourselves from Industrial Age behaviours that are no longer appropriate to Information Age living.

> *"At the centre of your being*
> *you have the answer; you know who you are and*
> *you know what you want."*
> *Lao Tzu*

~ Changing concepts of jobs ~

Before the 18th and 19th centuries, the concept of regular, full-time employment was unknown. It was only with the emergence of the factories and bureaucracies needed to oil the wheels of the newly industrialised society that people slowly – and painfully – embraced the notion of employment in one location, for one employer. And, unless you were incompetent or fraudulent, this meant the added security of a job for life. Hence we have become programmed to believe that jobs are the bedrock of a stable society. This is no longer the case. The same level of upheaval that necessitated freedom-loving, village-born artisans to uproot their families and go to work in William Blake's 'dark satanic mills' is being re-experienced;

although, ironically we are returning to the more flexible, home-based, talent-promoting kind of employment that constituted making a living centuries before. In cities, towns and villages all over the country people are operating their own service industries, from offering house- and pet-sitting to IT training and party planning. Far from the 'education in methodical habits' that mid-19th-century job-holders were instructed in, we are now faced with learning to become more flexible, creative, free thinking and marketable. From being workers and employees we are invited to become career entrepreneurs, business artists, and even 'Me PLC'.

However, we aren't going back to a pre-Industrial society where exchange of skills and bartering were the norm. Not all of us want to be freelance operators and many people will always prefer to be employees, with the added security that this offers. Small, medium-sized and big businesses will, of course, still exist, but even they aren't going to stay exempt for long from the major changes being made to the traditional model of employment. Some forward-thinking organisations are already 'de-jobbing', opening their doors 24 hours a day to people with no regular hours or confining job descriptions, whose output is monitored by results, not by clocking in and clocking out. Employees are becoming accountable to their project-team members rather than a conventional manager and, as anyone who has faced peer group criticism for not pulling their weight knows, this is a stronger incentive to buckle down and get the job done. Nowadays, staff jobs are synonymous with skills and competencies, rather than functions. There's a blending process going on that requires managers to learn to type because they are frequently using their laptops away from the traditional office, while well-organised, imaginative secretaries have the chance to put together a corporate event or otherwise demonstrate greater creativity than typing someone else's mind-numbing reports. This phenomenon is not restricted to one nation or continent, it is global. Even the Japanese obsession with lifetime employment is crumbling, with companies like Toyota creating a new category of temporary professional workers hired on a one-year contract basis.

Traditional jobs, with their rigid job descriptions, all too frequently force square pegs into round holes. However, today's new world of work offers many opportunities and a supportive environment for undertaking your heart's work.

- **Flexibility** The opportunity to work when you want to, where you want to; to no longer be tied to an office, which inevitably involves travelling on public transport or roads during the rush hour, spending all that time and money getting stressed out because of the inevitable delays (not to mention the cost). Flexible working – whether through job sharing, tele-working from home, hot desking (combining periods working from home with going into an office) or variable hours – will make it easier to manage work and family demands. This is particularly valuable at a time when a staggering 90 per cent of individuals surveyed said that their careers caused them to put work before their home and family life.

- **Choice** While working for larger companies offers opportunities to manoeuvre your career across different departments, the new way of working increases your chance to vary your employment, either within one area or across completely different ones. Whereas I have developed and diversified my latest career within the category of 'media and communication', my friend Paul, over the same period of time, has been a film develop- ment technician, salesperson, print specialist, media buyer, change agent for a multinational company and has now set up his own training consultancy. 'Pick and mix' portfolio working offers more opportunities to try out your skills in many different ways, all the time moving you towards the work you love to do.

- **Balance** Short-term contracts offer you the chance periodically to alternate work with leisure or study time, depending on your financial situation. Not being tied to the regular nine to five, five days a week, 48 weeks a year employment will make it easier, not just to juggle home and family, but will give you the opportunity to travel abroad for longer than a fortnight a year, to study for qualifications or just to have some stress-free, 'quality' time away from regular working demands. Most of us don't want to stop working, we just want to feel less pressurised. Having the chance to take regular, short breaks from work, because we aren't tied to one employer, will allow us to achieve that.

"Your past is not your potential. In any hour you can choose to liberate the future."
Marilyn Ferguson

~ The changing face of work: social and business reasons ~

So, how do *you* begin to reconcile this new working environment with the chance to do what you love for a living? The answer may lie in your childhood, as whatever you dreamed then of doing as an adult offers a major clue to uncovering the work you were born to do. Children have the most glorious dreams for themselves as far as working is concerned. They don't view work as something that is laborious, tedious, stressful and soul destroying in the way many adults do. That is because, with so little personal history, or past, they create their lives by looking forwards to the future. They want to have exciting working lives, adventurous ones, to save the planet, to look after people, to *enjoy* themselves. They don't make the differentiation between work and play because they haven't yet learned to compartmentalise their lives as adults do, nor do they put any limits on what they want to become. By using their imaginations to dream up their ideal job, children unwittingly benefit from one of the most effective strategies for harnessing success and coping with change: to be *pulled by the future* rather than being informed by the past.

But then what happens? They come up against parents and teachers who tell them to be realistic and give up any thoughts of being a rocket scientist or inventor. They go to see a careers guidance advisor (usually the physics teacher, who doesn't mind filling in a spare half day by doing this on the side!), who suggests they forget their desire to be an opera singer or actor and opt for something 'safe', such as a teacher or secretary or computer programmer. Alternatively, some ambitious parents manoeuvre their artistic children into the professions. When your father, grandfather and possibly great-grandfather before you have been doctors or lawyers then it takes a lot of guts to buck the trend at 15 and say you want to be a landscape gardener, hairdresser or journalist instead. The drip, drip, drip of messages such as: 'You can't do that' or 'Life's not like that', gradually extinguishes a young person's fire and passion to be what they truly want to be and so they find themselves doing jobs that other people think are best for them.

This is more of a widespread problem than you might think. A survey reported in a US popular psychology magazine revealed that up to 40 per cent of the population had 'drifted' into a career and less than a quarter had personally chosen their line of work. What underpins this sad state of affairs are attitudes that encourage you not to reach for the skies in case you find you can't get off the ground. And well-meaning adults genuinely don't want the young people under their care to be disappointed and discouraged. They think that it is best for teenagers to set their sights considerably lower and achieve whatever offers security, a reasonable income and a degree of status.

But what are we doing selling out on our dreams in order to make others feel more comfortable about giving up theirs? The inspirational spiritual author Marianne Williamson expressed this so elegantly in her book *A Return to Love*, thus:
'Our deepest fear is not that we are inadequate.
Our deepest fear is that we are powerful beyond measure.
It is our light, not our darkness, that most frightens us.
We ask ourselves, "who am I to be brilliant, gorgeous, talented, fabulous?"
Actually, who are you not to be?
You are a child of God. Your playing small doesn't serve the world.

There's nothing enlightened about shrinking so that other
people won't feel insecure around you.
We are all meant to shine, as children do.
We were born to make manifest the glory of God that is
within us.
It's not just in some of us; it's in everyone.
And as we let our own light shine, we unconsciously give
other people permission to do the same.
As we are liberated from our own fear, our presence
automatically liberates others.'

If only our children were given a copy of these words at
school and told not to give up their dreams simply because
someone else thinks they are unrealistic. It is the dreamers in
life who make such an enormous contribution to society.
Thankfully Thomas Edison, when developing the light bulb,
didn't think to himself: 'no one else has used a spider's web
or cheese, so perhaps I shouldn't either'. He went ahead and
tried them anyway when working his way through 10,000 different materials in order to find a filament that worked. If
Albert Einstein hadn't allowed himself to day-dream, chances
are he would not have postulated the nature of the universe
as being both finite and curved. As one of the greatest minds
of all time he didn't think it unusual to imagine himself rid-
ing on a sunbeam in order to conclude that on reaching the
'end' of the universe he was back where he had begun.

Of course you need to be pragmatic about what you do for
a living, but realism should follow the creativity of your original dream, not be your starting point. Unfortunately, in most
cases, people simply give up their dream at the first hurdle
because it didn't work out exactly as they wanted it to and,
having had their hopes dashed once, they decide to stick to
something safe in future. If you are prepared to be flexible, the
dream you had as a child can find its expression because ele-
ments of such dreams tell you something fundamental about
yourself and what, as a unique individual, you are here to do.

Ancient philosophers have taught that work should be an
expression of the inner self and, as such, not compartmen-
talised from the rest of our lives. Buddha introduced the

concept of 'Right Livelihood' as a natural expression of our innate creativity and unique gifts. This represents work as a way of being, an authentic demonstration of our inner self: one of the core messages of this book. Confucius echoed this sentiment when he said that the master of the art of living makes little distinction between work and play: he or she simply pursues a vision of excellence in whatever is done for a living.

There has never been a time in which the rate of change has accelerated so fast. And it is precisely because the world of work is changing so fundamentally that we all need to look to what *could be* rather than what *is*. Tomorrow's needs cannot be solved by yesterday's solutions. This is the perfect time to throw out old, preconceived notions of how work should be and how it fits in with the rest of our lives; and this book offers you the tools and techniques with which to confidently embrace those changes and, in the process, achieve greater creative expression, meaning and joy in your working life.

Most of us are resistant, to some degree, to the notion of change, but it is going to happen to you some day – whether you are prepared for it or not. Employers are beginning to recruit in very different ways than they did in the past, looking for individuals whose attitudes, as well as skills, fit the culture of the company, rather than going through the uphill struggle of moulding existing employees to fit the new paradigm (see Air Miles, page 34).

The notion of 'jobs for life' has largely been thrown out of the window, even in historically secure professions such as teaching, banking and the civil service. In an effort to reduce costs, organisations are choosing corporate anorexia: downsizing and out-sourcing, enforcing redundancies and early retirement on those people who no longer meet their requirements. The more enlightened companies are doing what they can to help their employees become employable: that is, to equip them with the skills they need to find work elsewhere, because they can't guarantee them jobs for longer than a few years. The parent-child relationship that most of us have had with our employers in the past is rapidly being replaced with an adult-adult relationship where each employee is expected to take responsibility for his or her career in the same way that governments are expecting members of society to become more responsible for their pensions and health care.

~ Case study: Air Miles ~

British Airways' most successful subsidiary, Air Miles, is an example of a company taking a very specific view of the attitudes they are seeking in employees, and the length of time people can expect to work for the company. They currently employ about 1,000 people, 80 per cent of whom work in call centres. This type of employment represents the biggest growth area in the UK, far exceeding that of the gas, steel and car industries combined. Currently, call-centre staff provide information, take bookings or try to sell you something. However, with the advent of digital television this is likely to change more to problem solving. Therefore Air Miles recognises the need to recruit individuals who want to be empowered.

Because of its specific culture, the company puts a strong value on honesty. Says Air Miles' director of people and culture, Larry Hochman:

'Explaining and preparing people for the new worlds of work begins at the recruitment stage, when we overtly say that all companies in the future will be taking people on for much shorter periods of time. Everybody who joins Air Miles understands that they do not have a job for life: on average, full-time employees stay for about three to three and a half years. We have created an environment of brutal honesty because while doubt is uncomfortable, certainty is ridiculous.

'Our culture empowers employees by making them more marketable for their next job, in exchange for adding value while they are with the company. Staff retention is a business holy grail that sets good people off on bad quests. The common belief is that recruiting is too expensive, but I would rather pay out money training new people than keep staff who are no longer passionate about their work and therefore can potentially lose us much more in terms of reduced customer service and satisfaction.

'Today's consumers want speed and ease of service. They don't want to be passed from pillar to post in their quest for information. They want to deal with individuals who can answer their queries and who have the confidence to make decisions on their own. That is why we try to hire people with passion and flexibility, the ability to manage ambiguity and the desire to be empowered. At Air Miles, customer service staff can use their discretion to refund miles or to give customers gifts up to the value of £200 without checking with a supervisor. In fact, there are only two layers between frontline staff and managing directors anyway.'

~ The changing patterns of work ~

Cary Cooper, Professor of Organisational Psychology at the Manchester School of Management (UMIST) pointed out in his 1997 RSA lecture on the psychological implications of the changing patterns of work that: 'The psychological contract between employer and employee in terms of "reasonably permanent employment for work well done" is being undermined, as more employees no longer regard their employment as secure and many more are engaged in part-time working.'
He reported that:

- The number of people employed by firms of more than 500 employees has slumped to just over a third of the employed population
- From 1984 to 1994 the number of men working part-time doubled
- 48 per cent of managers say their biggest worry is employability in the wider job market
- The UK shows the worst decline in employee satisfaction in terms of employment security of any of its European competitors: from 70 per cent satisfaction in 1985 to 48 per cent in 1995
- One in eight UK managers work more than 60 hours per week
- The annual cost to industry due to sickness absence has hit an all-time high of £12 billion.

As Cooper and Jackson predict in their handbook *Creating Tomorrow's Organisations*, most companies will only keep on a minority of full-time, permanent employees who work in conventional offices, preferring to buy in most of the skills they need on a contract basis from short-term or 'virtual' workers (that is, workers brought in for a specific project only, or who work via new technology as part of a virtual team). British Telecom estimates that by the millennium, 4 million people will work wholly or partly from home. This is the shape of things to come – a new revolution is upon us, just as mould breaking as the Industrial Revolution – and each of us has to prepare for that with new attitudes, beliefs and behaviours. However, there are many potentially positive outcomes in this new world of work, as you will discover further in Chapter Three (How much do you willingly embrace change?), but you will see them only if you choose to change your internal dialogue from: 'How can I avoid this?' to 'How can I take advantage of this?'

One of the most exciting opportunities offered by the new working environment is the chance to live your dream and make a living from a job that really fires you up and from which you gain immense pleasure. This book will help you find the kind of work you love to do, to prepare yourself for the future so that you can be confident of having the sort of attitude that today's and tomorrow's organisations are looking for, and weave some magic into your work so that it becomes a more inspiring aspect of your life. The techniques offered in the following chapters will help you decide whether to make a fresh choice and move to a more satisfying career, or stay where you are and find new purpose in your current workplace. This is even more important when you consider that you will probably need to work for much longer than your parents did. Whereas in the UK today there are 3.3 jobholders for every pensioner, this ratio will have dropped to just two by the year 2030. Unless the government allows the state pension system to completely grind to a halt, those who are fit and healthy enough to work will need to extend their working lives in order to fund the 15 million people expected to draw a state pension in the next 20 to 30 years.

Additionally, we are all living longer: 75 years for men and 80 years for women compared with 56 and 60 years respectively in 1928. How many of us who feel and look younger than our years want to vegetate around the house for decades, barely able to afford the occasional trip or little luxury? This is why so many 50-plus individuals in good physical and mental health are leaving full-time employment and replacing it with portfolio careers that are often quite different to what they did before: an illustration that age is no barrier to living your dream. However, *Working from the Heart* seeks to demonstrate that you don't have to wait until you are near retirement age to love what you do for a living.

~ Have a heart ~

Why 'work from the heart'? Why not continue to 'work from the head'? After all, business is 'head' driven, isn't it? In the traditionally male-dominated world of paid employment the attributes most applauded have included objectivity, hard logic, organisation, analysis and decision making, based on perceived bottom-line benefits. Yet what sort of impact has such a 'heartless' approach to work had on employees? They feel unloved, unappreciated, unhappy, unfulfilled, demotivated, resentful and – here's the crux of the matter for business – are also unproductive. Research into the impact of employee attitudes shows that companies with high levels of satisfaction and commitment enjoy increased performance in terms of profitability and productivity. Whereas unhappy workers suffer most from stress, fear, fatigue and demonstrate a marked decrease in creativity.

Business guru Tom Peters summed up the problem when he said: 'Store shelves groan under the weight of new products, but few have heart. Service offerings are about as lifeless. Most hotels, for example, spent the last decade buffing their customer service. The mechanics are better. Bravo. But the heart is usually absent: the sincere sense of "Welcome to my home" as opposed to "I've gotta remember to act like I care".'

Taking your heart to work is an alien concept for many because of the traditional meanings we have ascribed to that organ. The heart is seen as the female (business translation = weaker) domain; a 'soft option' wrapped up in emotion (business translation = lack of control). The heart is generally considered to be about children, relationships, love, poetry, soppy stuff, sensitivity, illogicality: in short, everything that is anathema to hard-headed business interests. Yet research coming out of the new scientific field of energy cardiology proves that putting your heart into your work is a vital ingredient that results in competitive advantage, both corporately and individually; but more importantly, would make the world a better place to be as well as to work. Unfortunately, 'Our people are our most valuable asset' remains an empty boast of many of today's organisations, who appear to want individuals who act with no more feeling than a computer. And this, ironically, is happening at a time when experts are stressing the need to capture the asset of 'emotional capital' on a company's balance sheet – representing the feelings, beliefs, perceptions and values of its employees – in order to sustain a competitive advantage.

"It is only with the heart
that one can see rightly;
what is essential is invisible to the eye."
Antoine de Saint-Exupéry

To understand the heart better, let's take a brief look at the science behind it. We're not just talking here about an organ that simply pumps blood around the body but about one that is an immensely powerful, dynamic, 'info-energetic' system. The heart is the body's main power generator, producing an electromagnetic field 5,000 times more powerful than that of the brain. With the aid of ECG equipment and spectrum analysis, scientists can measure the heart's electrical signals in every part of the human body, and know that they have an impact on every single cell. The heart connects and bonds with all other parts of the body in a way that the brain could never do, which is why it can be said that working from the head alone contributes to so much illness and disease in the form of heart failure, lowered immune systems and malignant cells.

The connection between the brain/mind and the heart is indisputable. You just have to think of an intimate moment with your lover, recall a frightening or embarrassing situation from your past, or simply bring to mind your child's first smile, word or steps, and your heart rate changes, often quite dramatically. This is because our sympathetic and parasympathetic wiring carries impulses from the brain to the heart, glands and other organs to speed up or slow down our responses as appropriate: the classic 'fight or flight' syndrome.

However, we have tended in the past to think of this link as being a one-way street, with the stimulus from the head affecting the heart, but not the other way round. Yet neurocardiologists have found a nerve pathway called the Baroreceptor system that originates in the heart and transmits electrical information from there to the brain. This system is said to be 'the only known nerve pathway which, when stimulated, can alter perceptions in the higher brain centres'. According to psychoneuroimmunologist Dr Paul Pearsall, 'The heart ... exerts at least as much control over the brain as the brain exerts over the heart.' This control includes the heart's production of a neuropeptide called Atrial Naturetic Factor (ANF), which is then transmitted throughout the body, linking particularly the emotional, memory and learning parts of the brain, the immune system, and the pineal gland, which relates to our rate of ageing and general energy levels. Evidence from the US National Institute of Mental Health suggests that the heart is actually the master controller of the body, organising its entire energy supply. What goes on in your heart will have a positive or negative effect on every other part of you: mentally, physically and spiritually.

When we feel love, joy and appreciation – all concepts attributed to a connection with the heart – they are translated into beneficial electrical energy or 'heart waves' with which every single cell in our bodies is bathed. Loving, caring individuals (and remember here that self-love and self-care are fundamental factors in this process) have lower levels of damaging stress hormones; have stronger immune systems which are flooded with the beneficial antibody Immunoglobulin A (IgA), our front-line defence against infections and disease; and have increased levels of norepinephrine, a chemical that helps to balance the nervous system, ensuring a lower risk of 'burn out'. It is not surprising, then, that people who love their work are healthier, more energised, take less days off sick and age less fast. Nor is it any coincidence that people with life-threatening conditions, including cancer, sometimes find that they heal spontaneously just by changing their jobs. In addition, because the heart's electrical energy acts as both a transmitter and receiver of radio waves, 'heart workers' – people who don't just operate from their heads – are more receptive to atmospheres between people, are more intuitive, sensitive and empathetic: that is, they are better communicators. Because such people are adept at recognising emotionally charged situations, they have the necessary awareness to choose to do something about them and hence make superior co-workers and employees.

But it is not just our mental and physical well-being that the heart contributes to through its two-way relationship with the brain/mind. Dr Pearsall, in his book *The Heart's Code*, believes the heart has an invaluable contribution to make to our consciousness through 'cellular memories'. He postulates that these cellular memories are the informational template of the soul and if only we could learn to silence the mind and be open to the heart's wisdom we would achieve a greater understanding of what our life is all about – what we are here for. Dr Pearsall calls the heart 'a spiritual recording chamber' containing a subtle code that, once deciphered through silence and contemplation, and a willingness for things not always to be rational or logical, allows us greater understanding of consciousness, human healing and our soul's purpose. It is only through listening to our hearts that we can begin the journey towards finding our mission in life, which embraces the work we do. Medical science is already puzzled by the fact that many people who die of heart disease have none of the common risk factors of a high cholesterol diet, obesity, smoking, or lack of exercise. We may be nearer than we think to finding scientific proof for the esoteric belief that our heart, through the spiritual energy it pumps in addition to its daily biochemical nutrients, tries to speak to us of love, including the self-love one experiences when engaged in work you feel passionate about, and weakens when it fails to be heard.

~ Robert's story ~

Robert is a 59-year-old film production accountant who started his working life as a tea boy at a film studio in South
London, UK. He says that had he been sent by his mother to
work in an electric light bulb factory, that would be the business he'd be in today. Robert achieves fulfilment in his work
by recognising what drives him personally and how that fits
with his professional life.

As a child, Robert wanted to be a lawyer, and dreamt of
the day he would pit his wits against the cleverest minds in
the country. However, his family's social and economic position meant that this was an impossibility and he gradually
worked his way into accountancy within the film industry.
Robert's was not an especially insecure childhood financially,
but he was strongly influenced by his parents' values of only
buying what you can afford at the time. He is very careful
with money and is driven by the need to be financially secure;
money means independence to him, allowing him to turn
down work he is not interested in and not having to work
with people he doesn't like.

Robert's personal fascination – his passion – for handling
money accurately causes him to treat the company's finances
in the same way as his own, which far exceeds what is expected of him professionally. Last year he handled £10 million
worth of funding and at the end his accounts weren't a penny
out. He's also been known to find a discrepancy of 3p within
a turnover of £250,000.

Robert admits his attention to detail is born out of an inferiority complex from his childhood, in which he seeks to
demonstrate that – despite a film agent's or studio boss's better education or privileges in life – he is cleverer than they are.
He loves to hear employers utter the words, 'What would you
do?' and will always try to offer them several alternatives to
problems, such as what to do about the added cost of making
up lost days' filming. His work has to be about problem solving rather than simply checking figures or moving sums from
one account to another. He is not interested in money for its
own sake but the challenges that accompany it. Robert
regards himself as an investigator rather than an accountant,

in which he loves to show people how to get more out of their available capital or how to produce the same for less cost.

Always looking for the game or puzzle is how Robert copes with the tedious side of his occupation. In the same way that he challenges himself to do the 'across' clues first in a crossword puzzle, before attempting the 'down' clues, Robert says he could enjoy sticking stamps on envelopes: he'd simply challenge himself to find a way to do it quicker or more efficiently.

~ Be whatever you choose to be ~

Let me conclude this chapter by introducing a concept that will be developed further in Chapter Two: that you can be whatever you choose to be or think you are. This is the message of a story called 'The Rabbi's Gift', which I heard re-told by the inspiring speaker Sir Benjamin Zander, and which can be found in the prologue of M Scott Peck's *The Different Drum*.

One day the abbot of a monastery, which had fallen on hard times, was discussing, with a nearby rabbi, what could be done to save it. The rabbi shrugged and said he had no answer: it seemed people just didn't want to visit religious places any more. Just as the abbot was leaving, the rabbi mysteriously added that he believed the Messiah to be one of the holy men living at the monastery.

When the abbot relayed this back to the other four monks, all of them were taken aback. What could the rabbi have meant by this? While remaining incredulous that the Messiah could be one of them, the monks' attitudes and behaviour began to change. Each one started to treat each other and himself with greater respect: just in case the rabbi's prediction turned out to be true after all. As they changed, the atmosphere of the monastery also changed, so much so that people who otherwise would have just passed by started to visit the old monks. In time, the monastery began to resound with the sound of praying and singing. Local youngsters who saw how joyous this life could be decided they wanted to become monks too, and joined the order. And so the abbot got the thriving, vibrant monastery he had wished for.

Whatever you think has a profound effect, not just on yourself but on your environment. However you think about yourself determines how other people treat you. We are now going to find out how to turn your thoughts to your advantage in the next chapter.

---

*"For if you bake bread with indifference, you bake a
bitter bread that feeds but half man's hunger.
And if you grudge the crushing of the grapes,
your grudge distils a poison in the wine."*
Kahlil Gibran

 **Your action list from this chapter**

Write down at least six things that you intend to do now – ie, today
not tomorrow – based on what you have learned in this chapter.

1

2

3

4

5

6

Will the real YOU please stand up?

"It is far more important that one's life should be perceived than that it should be transformed; for no sooner has it been perceived, than it transforms itself of its own accord."
Maurice Maeterlinck

~ Anne's story ~

Everyone at work thought Anne was totally career focused. She had excelled at university, risen rapidly through the ranks of various advertising agencies and had become a director with her current company. She seemed to attract men with the same sort of work ethic as herself, which was why none of her relationships lasted more than a few months: after all, two people working 60 hours a week were hardly likely to find time for each other. None of Anne's colleagues felt they ever really knew her, although she was well liked and respected for her creativity. No one at the agency thought of discussing domestic matters with Anne and she never talked about a home life or having children. Not until – highly stressed and on the brink of burn out – she went to see a psychotherapist and the real Anne came pouring out.

An only child, Anne had been under constant pressure from her ambitious parents to succeed, which, according to their definition, meant having a highly paid career. She had been indoctrinated at an early age by her mother (a GP) that having children squandered a woman's intellect and prevented her from living life to the full. Frightened by her mother's caustic personality, Anne found that life was easier if she did what everyone else expected of her. She had become a workaholic in order to avoid facing herself and the emotional void in her life. Once on this treadmill of self-deception, Anne found it impossible to get off, until her warring body and mind forced the issue. She frequently suffered from exhaustion and depression and began to worry that she might have M.E.

The truth, as her therapist soon found out, was that Anne was desperately unhappy with her work. She detested what she regarded as the trivial nature of her job, feeling she was contributing little to society through devising increasingly surreal campaigns to sell more consumer products. What Anne had always wanted to do was to work with children, find her soul mate and raise a large family, ensuring none of them experienced the loneliness of her own childhood.

Anne had waited until she was 36 years of age, and had despaired of ever settling down and having children, before she chose to become 'authentic'. Her parents, colleagues and all but a few close friends thought she was having a complete mental breakdown when Anne announced she was turning her back on her highly paid career to train as a teacher. Yet no one who saw this completely transformed woman in the months that followed could have doubted that Anne had at last found her mission in life.

How much of that story can you relate to? Perhaps you have managed to avoid the kind of serious physical or mental illness that many individuals like Anne have to face, which forces them to reassess their lives according to their own values, beliefs and desires. Whenever we are at war with ourselves expect battles – and casualties – because it's a no-win situation; that casualty will always be you. This incongruence between the person we present to the world at work and who we are outside of it, is illustrated in many different ways, although the underlying reason generally boils down to one thing: low self-esteem.

Anne's story illustrates two classic self-esteem issues that need to be addressed before any of us can begin to live a happy, integrated life:

1 Her belief that she was unworthy of happiness; that no one would love, accept or employ her if they saw the 'real' Anne, and

2 That life is all about self-sacrifice; in order to please other people – be that a partner, parent, colleague or boss – she must ignore her own needs.

~ Self-esteem ~

Self-esteem is a crucial factor, not only in finding work that you love to do, but in making yourself employable in the new world of work. It is defined as:

● Valuing yourself as a unique individual
● Having confidence in your ability to cope with life's challenges
● Accepting responsibility for your thoughts and actions
● Acknowledging your right to have wants and needs
● Respecting your desire to be successful and happy.

The roots of this near epidemic of low self-esteem – particularly for individuals who have, or are experiencing unemployment – is a complicated mix of nature and nurture. On the nurture side, low self-esteem is the sum total of the negative causes and effects that have accrued throughout our lives, principally through our relationships with others. It shows itself in a variety of different ways (see Petra's story, next page) but generally has its roots in allowing other people's demands – parents, early carers, siblings, lovers, colleagues – to negate your own wants, needs and happiness. Because of this you soon lose a sense of your own identity. The emptiness that accompanies low self-esteem arises because your soul or spirit no longer feels it has a place to call its own. It is manifested when you allow other people to occupy your mind and body through dictating what you should think, value and how you should behave.

Most of us journey through life battling between our two selves: the one we were born to be, frequently called the Whole Self, Higher Consciousness or Spiritual Self; and the one we have learned to be, the Ego or Personality. The Ego is a mask that we wear to cover up the fact that we have lost connection with our true identity. The Swiss psychoanalyst Carl Gustav Jung called the Ego 'the persona', which comes from the Latin word for 'theatre mask'. It is only when you are prepared to remove this mask that you will be able to rediscover your true self or spirit and draw into your life the work that is best suited to it. We are all born whole, complete and perfect for the mission we were born to complete, it's just that we aren't aware of that 100 per cent of the time. The ugly duckling story is a perfect analogy of this: the ugly duckling was a swan all along; he just never realised it.

The problem when you force yourself to go through life wearing a mask is that it will either slip, giving people an almighty shock when it does, or will cause you to be extremely unhappy as you exhibit attitudes and behaviours that do not reflect your true beliefs. This happens a lot within relationships when, anxious to find a partner – *any* partner – we portray ourselves as the other person would like us to be. Then, after we have hooked our catch, and gradually begin to feel safe enough with them, we allow our true nature to show through. Unfortunately this frequently creates deep rifts within the relationship as our partner bemoans the fact that we have 'changed' and are no longer the person they fell in love with. But we haven't changed at all, we've just not been totally honest with ourselves or them because we were so desperate to achieve a particular objective.

The same is true in the workplace. By allowing ourselves to be indoctrinated to believe that jobs are scarce, that it's a buyer's market and we should take almost anything that is offered to us, we say all the things we know a prospective employer wants to hear, and pay the price when we are stuck in a job that is fine for our minds, but not our hearts.

There's a fine line, particularly confusing when your level of self-worth is low to start off with, between knowing when someone is manipulating you towards something you don't want to do and a job that others – from an objective perspective – can see you have a natural affinity for. It is always important to respond to your gut instincts, those messages from your soul that tell you: 'Yes, this is a perfect expression of my unique gifts and talents' or 'No, my heart isn't really in this work'. But sometimes well-meaning friends or co-workers can help steer you in the right direction.

~ Petra's story ~

Petra belonged to a small group of in-house trainers working within a major multinational leisure company. When the team was originally set up, the members assessed both their own and their colleagues' talents in order to decide where they could best be deployed. The rest of the group felt that Petra's particular strengths lay in the area of organisation and that she would be the ideal person to arrange the vital, behind-the-scenes activities that ensured workshops actually happened and were successfully managed. Petra was very unhappy at this suggestion and argued strongly to be an active member of the training team. She wanted to run courses, not be in charge of 'just' booking the venues, preparing the materials and administering the delegates. A number of her colleagues felt that this was a mistake as Petra didn't have sufficient depth of knowledge of the course material, had experienced a number of interpersonal problems with delegates in the past and was thought not to have the extraversion required of workshop leaders. However, her depth of feeling persuaded them to let her do the job she wanted and Petra began facilitating.

It didn't take long for problems to crop up. Delegates consistently rated Petra low in comparison with her colleagues, she found that she didn't enjoy the work as much as she thought she would and was overwhelmed by the amount of new knowledge she was expected to absorb.

The turning point came when someone suggested that Petra take charge of organising a major one-week training course abroad. She was brilliant at it. Her colleagues were full of praise for the way her efforts had enabled them to concentrate on what they were best at: delivering training in a fun and compelling way. Petra's belief in her abilities, which had taken a considerable dent because of her perceived failure at a job she thought she had wanted, rose considerably and she agreed to take on the role full-time.

How to play to your strengths, not to your understrengths (a better word, don't you agree, than 'weaknesses'?) is developed further in Chapter Four. However, the point illustrated here is that Petra's low self-esteem required her to be in the visible, high-profile, more 'glamorous' role of facilitating – even though she wasn't particularly good at it and it was causing her considerable unhappiness. In her heart she was the consummate administrator. Her ego just needed to be reminded of that.

"Knowing other people is intelligence,
knowing yourself is wisdom.
Overcoming others takes strength,
overcoming yourself takes greatness."
Lao Tzu, **The Tao Te Ching**

~ Responsibilities and choices ~

The idea that we are responsible for the meanings we place on our lives and that we can re-frame them if we choose to do so is a challenging one to grasp and I admit that I have tussled with it most of my life. However, Viktor Frankl's *Man's Search for Meaning* offers a fresh and empowering perspective to hold on to. A Jew, Frankl endured years of unspeakable horror in the Nazi concentration camps during World War II, places you would think would be guaranteed to cause one to become spiritually decimated by days, months and years of man's inhumanity to man. Yet what Frankl's story demonstrates is that even when nothing else remains at an external level, there is the 'last of human freedoms': the ability to 'choose one's attitude'. As Frankl wrote: 'Woe to him who saw no more sense in his life, no aim, no purpose and therefore no point in carrying on. He was soon lost ... What was really needed was a fundamental change in our attitude toward life. We had to learn ourselves, and furthermore we had to teach the despairing men, that it didn't really matter what we expected from life, but rather what life expected from us.'

Frankl's experience is an extreme example of how we choose between experiencing anger, fear and despair, or love, happiness and community. Believing that reality is imposed upon us externally is a position well known to the Ego (an acronym for Everything Good's Outside). Hence we decide to wait for the 'right' job, the 'right' relationship, the material possessions that we think will make us happy, all the while neglecting to take control of our internal environment: the

way we think about things. We are supported in this view by
orthodox science that suggests the observer is separate from,
and therefore has no impact on, the observed. Yet when we
come to look at the discoveries made in quantum physics
(explained in detail in Chapter Seven) you will find that atomic
matter – the universal building block of life – changes according to how the observer chooses to observe it. That is why resculpting your life involves the art of changing your mind
about what is 'real'. Put simply, whatever you focus on you
will find in your life – because, well, that's what you've
focused on!

~ Many lives, many missions ~

Many ancient philosophies and religions embrace the notion
of reincarnation: that our spirits have lived many lives in the
past and will do so again in the future. Reincarnation was
accepted by the ancient Egyptians, who prepared their dead
for their journey to the next life with food, ornaments, gold
and other earthly possessions. Reincarnation is an integral
part of two major world religions, Hinduism and Buddhism,
plus is accepted by Sikhism, Sufism and certain cabbalistic
Jewish sects. The one notable exception to the conviction that
our spirits journey through countless lifetimes is modern
Christianity, which is surprising since one of its fundamental
beliefs is the resurrection of Jesus Christ. Christianity's non-
acceptance of reincarnation can be traced back to the 6th
century AD when Emperor Justinian decreed it to be a sin to
believe in the pre-existence of souls. This was in direct contradiction to the belief of Origen, described by St Jerome as
'the greatest teacher of the Church after the apostles'. Origen's
view was that: 'Every soul ... comes into the world strengthened by the victories or weakened by the defeats of its
previous life. Its place in this world ... is determined by its
previous merits or demerits. Its work in this world determines
its place in the world which is to follow this ...'
    Reincarnation expert Roy Stemmen offers a lovely analogy
of why our souls take on this seemingly endless journey of
reincarnation, when he writes: 'The rough and tumble of life
on earth, with all its excitements and pitfalls, seems to be a

valuable "classroom" for us to learn lessons, and it also seems logical that we might have to pass through many classrooms before we are ready to graduate.'

This concept is explored further when we look at how to deal with relationship difficulties with co-workers; see Chapter Seven (Are your working relationships making you unhappy?). It can also help with challenges such as periods of unemployment. Viktor Frankl's advice to his fellow concentration-camp inmates was to look upon suffering as a task, with hidden opportunities for achievement; a theme that is presented time and time again in mythological tales across all cultures.

From a spiritual perspective, our lives provide us with daily challenges – primarily through our relationships with others – that constantly test our self-belief, motivations and our faith in the ability to handle any task. By overcoming the penalty of low self-esteem, we begin to peel away the onion-like layers that hide our ultimate goal: authenticity. If you have spent your life battling against low self-esteem, in all its guises, then it may help you to look at the bigger picture and ask yourself: 'What are these challenges teaching me?' By doing this you can choose to accept that whatever makes you uncomfortable or unhappy is a potential source of growth and development and see life as an adventure, instead of a battle. Because if it is a constant battle, then that usually indicates you are at war within yourself.

Life liberally offers 'signposts' on our journey towards the authentic self, each of which need to be acknowledged and acted upon. These include:

- Strong, gut feelings; a compelling urge to do something completely 'out of character'
- Bouts of depression which can indicate a major discrepancy between how we think our life should be and how it actually is
- Working obsessively, not because we love what we do, but in order to avoid facing the problems in the rest of our lives
- Acute stress and its debilitating symptoms
- Extreme tiredness, particularly mental rather than physical exhaustion

- Illnesses that are now regarded as often having psychological roots, such as skin conditions, cancers, allergies, digestive and elimination problems, and back pain
- A feeling of emptiness and purposeless about life generally
- When your achievements – particularly material accomplishments – no longer hold any meaning for you (the classic 'mid-life crisis') and you start to ask 'Is this all there is?'
- Becoming addicted to alcohol, cigarettes, food, or drugs (recreational and/or prescribed)
- Always needing to be with people, keeping yourself busy with tasks and disliking periods of silence
- Recurring dreams about masks, animals and nakedness: these are all symbols that your subconscious throws up to encourage you to be more your instinctive self rather than hiding it from the world
- Underachievement at work, a form of subconscious self-sabotage.

These are all messages from your soul informing you that the door to a better life only opens when you knock on the inside. Life is immensely challenging, painful and impermanent, but we don't have to be beaten or demeaned by it. You can always take the view of the late Achaan Chah Subato, a Thai monk, who, when asked how he could be happy in such a world as ours, replied (my italics):

'Someone gave me this glass, and I really like this glass. It holds my water admirably, and it glistens in the sunlight. I touch it and it rings. One day the wind may blow it off my shelf or my elbow may knock it from the table. *I know this glass is already broken, so I enjoy it immensely.*'

The following exercises are designed to help you begin valuing your contribution to life, to enhance your confidence so that you can better cope with whatever challenges you are faced with, to show you that your needs and wants can be met and that you deserve and can achieve lasting success and happiness. They are particularly relevant if, in your list of personal needs (see Introduction, page 18), you place a high priority on: influence and power, reputation, support/loyalty of manager/boss, feedback on performance, being appreciated, or a feeling of being involved. These are all external validations which suggest that you habitually look outside yourself to measure your worth as a human being.

The truth is, you are a wonderful, talented, whole, unique and valuable individual in every moment of your existence; believe that wholeheartedly and none of those personal needs will have the same appeal to you.

Obviously a whole book (if not an entire library) could be dedicated to helping you understand yourself better and this chapter only scratches the surface and points you in the right direction. Many of the books listed in Further Reading (see page 187) offer excellent further guidance on living a more authentic life.

"At mid-life, a man or woman feels an inner siren call like an old memory. No matter how long and how faithful we have served we suddenly remember our former intuitions for a possible life."
David Whyte, **The Heart Aroused**

~ Preparation guidelines ~
for visualisation and meditation

Find a quiet area where you will be undisturbed for at least the next 30 minutes.

- Lock the door or put up a Do Not Disturb sign as appropriate.
- Take the telephone off the hook.
- Make sure you are warm and comfortable, but that there is also good ventilation.
- Try to wear loose clothing or at least nothing that will distract you because it is too tight or irritating.
- Find a position – either sitting or lying down – with which you feel most comfortable. It is necessary to remain in the same position for the duration of the exercise, so make sure it is one that won't cause you backache or stiffness.
- If you decide to burn a scented candle or incense to enhance the atmosphere, make sure you really like the smell and it isn't going to make the room too smoky. Place a jug of water nearby to maintain moisture levels.
- Have a glass of water or fruit juice to drink when you have completed your visualisation or meditation.
- Make sure you have been to the toilet/bathroom before commencing.

"The best way to get people to venture into
unknown terrain is to make it desirable
by taking them there in their imaginations."
Professor Noel M Tichy,
University of Michigan Business School

✍ Exercise: Be your own best friend

Make a list of all the things you expect or desire other people to do for you. This is a general exercise around getting to know yourself and, as such, need not be confined to work issues. Here is an example:

Felicity had recently split up with her married boyfriend, angry at the limited time they could spend together. She believed she loved him but knew in her heart that she could never share a man with his wife and was uncomfortable with the thought of breaking up his marriage. However, there were things that Dan had done for her that Felicity missed, and this loss was preventing her from moving on. After a painful couple of weeks in which Felicity was frequently in tears, a friend suggested that instead of focusing on what she was no longer getting from Dan, she should focus on what she could do for herself. Felicity made the following 'to do' list, most of it based on activities, she realised, that she had always expected a man to provide for her. After several months of looking after herself Felicity was not only much happier but attracted a number of interesting – and single – admirers. Felicity committed herself to:

● Buying herself a beautiful bunch of flowers every week
● Going to Ceroc (French 'jive') dancing classes where she didn't need a partner and would meet new people
● Sending herself loving e-mails and leaving little notes to herself around the house
● Treating herself to her favourite food, lovingly prepared and eaten in candlelight as if she were with a lover
● Looking in the mirror first thing every morning to tell herself, 'I love you'
● Treating herself to an aromatherapy massage every fortnight so she could experience the healing touch of another person.

Now make your own list of at least ten 'nice' things to do for yourself, then determine to act on it – right now. Remember, most of the things that you want or need from other people you can also give to yourself: from compliments to orgasms.

✑ Exercise: Give to receive

This is a very powerful variation on the previous exercise which acknowledges the fact that we are all linked energetically to everyone else (a concept explained in more detail in Chapter Seven), particularly those who frequently impact our lives physically, emotionally, or spiritually. That is why gestures of kindness, generosity, or love come back to you manifold.

All too frequently, whatever we are looking for from others we are failing to give out ourselves. Think carefully about what you feel is missing in your life (either based on the list from the previous exercise, or a new one) and then offer that from your heart, without expecting anything in return.

- If you want compliments and praise while you are working on your self-esteem, focus on praising others
- If you feel there is no one there for you, find out if there's a local children's or elderly persons' home that would appreciate some help for a couple of days a month
- If you wish someone to recognise your worth at work and promote you, consider whose career you could help, either with a practical gesture or a good word in the right place
- Find something good to say about everyone you meet – and tell them
- Write a card expressing your gratitude to a friend or member of your family for past kindnesses, or just for being who they are, and send it
- Accept no invitations without taking a gift from yourself, even if it is a single flower, or a kind word. Then just watch how quickly people start wanting to do things for you.

Ironically, the more you do for others the better you feel about yourself and the reward of getting something back becomes less of a necessity. What you give to yourself when you do this is a priceless gift: the gift of self-love.

✍ Exercise: Self-acceptance

The ancient Chinese recognised that there are two opposing but complementary forces in all things, which they termed 'yin' and 'yang'. That is how life is; we need to experience the dark to appreciate the light, and the negative to appreciate the positive. As the saying goes, 'It takes both sunshine and rain to make a rainbow'. Similarly, each of us is a complex combination of strengths and understrengths; the things we like about ourselves and those we dislike; talents we are proud to own and those we prefer to keep hidden – even from ourselves. Jung called this our shadow side, 'the thing a person has no wish to be'. The problem is, our shadow is part of us and, while it can be suppressed, it cannot be got rid of without destroying our whole self in the process. We cope with this dilemma by projecting our faults on to other people so that they are the ones who are boastful, aggressive, impractical, secretive, deceitful – not ourselves. As Jung suggested, the only way to view the world differently and be at peace within yourself – and with others – is to accept your shadow side, to 'own' it and come to terms with the fact that's just the way life is.

This exercise requires you to be totally honest with yourself and articulate those aspects of your nature, your personality, that you would rather not admit to. This is extremely important, because your relationship with your Self acts as a mirror for every other relationship you have. If you cannot be wholly happy with who you are, you will never be wholly happy with what you do or who you are with. To become a Whole Self means accepting your completeness, which includes 'you' when you are good, 'bad', or indifferent.

Find a quiet, relaxing place and time when you will not be disturbed. Then start to write down all the things about yourself that you really don't like. As you do this, thoughts might come into your head that haven't cropped up before: these are suggestions from your subconscious that want to join in the game too, so don't discount them. Just to make you feel a bit better about this, here is a part of my list: suspicious, impulsive, oversensitive, arrogant, insecure, inconsiderate.

Now you might wonder, having got a rather scary list in front of you, how – apart from 'owning' these attributes – this might relate to finding the work that you love. Well, in the same way that we need a shadow side as well as a light side, we can find a positive spin on every negative part of life, if we choose to look for it. I have recognised that my own shadow side provides me with certain qualities that are crucial to being a successful freelance journalist. My suspicious nature causes me not to trust things people tell me so I look for verification from other sources, which makes me a very thorough researcher. My impulsiveness has prompted me to take advantage of opportunities that would have evaporated had I thought about them for too long, added to my rich experience of life and taught me to take responsibility for my actions. My oversensitivity to criticism has made me more of a perfectionist; I don't always manage to get things right first time, but I do my very best to ensure that I meet deadlines and write clean copy that requires the minimum of editing.

Get the picture? Now think about all the so-called negative qualities written on your list and look at their positive potential. What does this tell you about the kind of employment, environment and colleagues that you need in order for your shadow side to be a useful asset?

Finally, I suggest you take your list and write at the top of the page: I accept myself for being ... and pin it up where you can look at it on a daily basis.

✍ Exercise: Creating the future You

Quantum physics (explained in greater depth in Chapter Seven) offers scientific validation of something we know innately: that life often seems contradictory. Susan Jeffers' book *Feel the Fear and Do It Anyway* outlines this perfectly: your reality partly consists of what is happening for you right now (feel the fear: ie, 'be'); but it is also made up of endless possibilities (do it anyway: ie, take action and create your future – 'become') depending on what it is you are creative enough to imagine.

That is why no work around who you are is complete without also taking into account who you would like to be. This is not to be confused with being dissatisfied with yourself, it's rather a case of re-invention, which celebrities such as Madonna, David Bowie and Cher have excelled at throughout their careers in order to adapt and remain successful in the highly competitive world of pop music. Our bodies re-invent themselves continually: we get a new stomach lining every five days, a new skin approximately every four weeks, a completely different liver every six weeks and a fresh skeleton four times a year, so why should we find it so hard to change our minds?

Follow the preparation guidelines for visualisation and meditation work outlined on page 54. Inhale deeply through your nose and fully exhale as slowly as you can. Repeat this three times. Keep your breathing slow and steady throughout this exercise. Now close your eyes and imagine you are reading a newspaper dated some way in the future, and have suddenly come upon the obituary pages. As you read the page relating to an elderly individual who passed away peacefully you realise that you are reading about yourself. What would you want that report to say? In it several of your friends, a member of your family, a work colleague and someone from your local community have been asked to write something about you. This is your imaginary exercise and you are able to influence their opinions. In what way would you want to be described in terms of your character, how you treated people, your service to the community, your worth as a friend, partner, parent or sibling?

Fix in your mind the sort of adjectives you would want these people to use about you. When you feel it is appropriate (and take as long as you like), slowly bring yourself back to the present time and open your eyes. Take a small sip of water to ground yourself. Jot down on a piece of paper the words and phrases you remember reading in your obituary. Now look at yourself honestly and ask yourself whether that future scenario is consistent with what people would say about you today. If not, what are the differences? How can you make these changes? Remember that change involves small, gradual, incremental steps. No one is asking you to effect a complete personality change overnight. But if you are committed to being thought of in the future in a different way – major or minor – than you are thought of today, then it is never too soon to take that first step.

✍ Exercise: Your Life Line

Buy a roll of plain lining paper from a wallpaper supply shop and, unrolling it as you go along, mark a line in the centre, widthways, like this.

Starting at the left-hand edge, begin by describing your earliest memories. Happy memories are to be written above the central line with the best ones near the top of the sheet; unhappy memories should be described below the line, again positioning them so that the ones you consider to be the worst are outlined along the lower edge of the paper. Include all your peak experiences, from academic achievements at school and college, success in learning a new skill or hobby, making friends with supportive, loving individuals, to the jobs you found most absorbing and satisfying. Be particularly careful to chart all your work experiences, even the ones you'd prefer to forget about (I have a few of these of my own). These are usually the ones that are most instructive when you come to analyse them.

Outline those life experiences that saddened or disappointed you or are otherwise connected in your memory with negative emotions. Take as much space as you need to describe each of these events fully, exploring both their meaning to you at the time and how you feel about them subsequently. It is important to give this exercise as much time and attention as you can as you will be using your 'peaks and troughs' Life Line in later chapters.

It is unlikely you will complete this in one sitting and you may want to work on it while reading this book for the first time, and then go back to engage in the other exercises when your Life Line has been completed.

As you do this exercise, and particularly when you have finished it, be aware of any themes that are threaded through your life. You might like to reflect on:

● The kind of people (if any) who were connected with particularly happy or unhappy experiences

- The kind of environments – your physical surroundings, the atmosphere, aesthetics or level of comfort – that caused you greatest happiness
- The type of activities you engaged in that determined whether you considered an event happy or unhappy
- The degree to which you had free choice and freedom of expression in each of these life events
- The common factors between experiences that made you feel special, loved, that life has a purpose, that you have a valuable contribution to make to the world
- Your degree of perseverance in, say, being a long-serving member of a club, or maintaining contact with friends who moved to another location and how you felt about that.

This list is not exhaustive. By acting like a detective, looking for as many links as possible between all the positive and then all the negative events in your life, you will undoubtedly come up with your own areas of investigation. Once you have analysed your life in this way, all the time asking yourself what made the difference between an experience that was happy and fulfilling or unhappy and distressing for you, write down what this tells you about the kind of person you are. Ask yourself:

1 What internal and external states do you need in place before you experience satisfying events?
2 To what extent do other people's opinions or actions impact on your ability to feel loved and content?
3 What expectations did you have about your life when you were young and to what extent have these been realised?
4 What role do you feel most comfortable with and why? Does this suggest the 'real' you?

There are no right or wrong answers to an exercise like this. Nor is there a conclusion one can reach, other than to be aware of the insights you will gain from exploring what makes you tick. Make sure you keep your notes about what your Life Line reveals about your inner self as you will need to refer to them later in this book.

~ Calling Lady Luck ~

Luck has been called a self-fulfilling prophecy: that is, if you believe in it – and think of yourself as a 'lucky' person – the more likely you are to experience it. It is true that some people who are innately positive in their approach to life, consider themselves to be lucky and generally happy, experience more fortunate lives. There are also those who focus on their goals like a laser beam and achieve the career they want, the partner they desire and the material possessions they covet. Are these people luckier than the rest of us? Not according to author Max Gunther, who researched the subject of luck and identified five characteristics that 'luck-prone' people possess. None of them is particularly mysterious or magical. They are:

● Consistently networking: making as many varied contacts as possible
● Acting on hunches or gut feelings
● Taking calculated risks; fortune, after all, favours the brave
● Cutting your losses quickly: that is, getting out of deteriorating situations as soon as possible
● Nurturing pessimism: that is, not taking an unrealistically optimistic approach to life.

Given this list, I think we can all learn to be lucky, don't you?

~ Be in the flow ~

An American psychologist named Mihaly Csikszentmihalyi has spent many years researching what he calls 'flow experiences': those moments of effortless action that have been variously described by others as ecstasy, rapture, 'being in the zone' and 'when time stands still'. For those of you for whom the word passion feels inappropriate, 'flow' may be a more meaningful and compelling concept. You know flow experiences have happened to you when you become lost in a favourite activity that requires deep concentration and challenges your existing skills. These activities vary from person to person and can include listening to music, constructing a complicated toy or puzzle, cooking a meal, performing surgery, playing an instrument, or knitting a jumper. What marks these moments as different from others, Csikszentmihalyi found, was that they usually involve clear goals and rules of performance: you know when you have accomplished them.

As you work your way through the rest of this book, note any flow experiences that you may have. Jot down what they were, where they occurred, how you felt at the time (your emotional state) and anything else that may be relevant to helping you repeat it. Csikszentmihalyi found that flow frequently occurs at work but rarely during passive leisure activities such as watching television. He offers some clues as to how you can increase your flow experiences at work by suggesting that they occur when you are emotionally involved in your job and anyone impacted by it.

Examples include store staff who pay genuine attention to serving the needs of their customers; administrative staff who constantly ask 'Could this job be done better, faster, more efficiently?'; doctors who regard each patient as an individual with unique needs and take the time to really listen to what others have to say; teachers who go out of their way to bring their subjects to life for their pupils; writers who care about the impact their work will have on their readers.

Anything that transforms a routine task into one that makes a difference – to you or to others – (see also Personal Signatures, page 99) will boost your chances of experiencing flow. To what extent could you inject this into your life right now?

"I think most of us are torn.
We have at least two people at war in our body.
One person wants to retire and grow fabulous
tomatoes, and the other wants to stand up on a
pedestal and be worshipped and get bigger and
bigger and bigger until she explodes."
Bette Midler

~ Nine steps to the work you love ~

You have to know who you are before you can develop a plan to get what you want. Someone who is a home-bird at heart and places a high value on family commitments is hardly likely to be happy as an international travel writer, for example. If your passion is amateur dramatics or playing in the local cricket team, how does this stack up against your desire for a career in newspapers, the film industry or the restaurant business, with very long, unsocial hours. When would you ever find the time to attend rehearsals or play matches? In Chapter Four (What do you really want to do?), you will pull together these and the other exercises in this book into a means of helping you uncover your life's purpose and hence the kind of work that will help you best express this. In the meantime, here are nine further steps to take you closer to making the work you love a reality:

1 **Acknowledge and love yourself** for who you are and, in that state of self-acceptance, determine to make slow, incremental changes to improve upon characteristics that you feel are holding you back. For example, accept that all of us have a degree of low self-esteem, but we can learn to become more self-nurturing and confident in a Universe – a higher power or influence – that wants us to be happy.

2 **Face your fears.** Someone once said, 'My life has been made up of misery, mishap and unhappiness, most of which have never happened.' How many times have you been afraid to say something challenging to someone – either in a work or family context – and found that, when you plucked up the courage to do so, the experience wasn't as bad as you thought it would be?

3 **Take responsibility for your life.** As Fritz Perls, the founder of Gestalt therapy says: 'You can always blame the parents if you want to play the blaming game and make the parents responsible for all your problems. Until you are willing to let go of your parents, you continue to conceive of yourself as a child.' Remember, sending children to work – down the mines, up chimneys or behind dangerous machinery – was an Industrial Revolution activity; it's not appropriate for the Information Age. Embrace your adulthood wholeheartedly.

4 **Be prepared to analyse your life** in a detached, objective way, rather like a detective piecing together the threads of someone else's life. Use the Life Line exercise (see page 60) to help you detect patterns of behaviour and attitudes that you may or may not wish to re-visit. One of the most challenging things for us to accept about ourselves is that we are human *beings* not human *doings*. Sometimes it's enough just to bring a desire for change into our consciousness and leave the Universe to take care of the details.

5 **Find positive role models** who you admire, either living and known (or unknown) to you, or characters from history or mythology. The wonderful thing about your imagination is that you can use it for any circumstance. If you believe your heart's desire has found similar expression in someone's life, read about what they did, how they coped with challenges – and day-dream about the advice they would give you to become more authentic.

6 **Be realistic and take the appropriate action.** If you want to be more assertive then book yourself on an assertiveness course. If you want to have a more active social life then explore what it is that will motivate you to widen your circle of friends, be it through a dancing class, an adult education course, or a singles club, if that is appropriate. If you want to set up your own small business, let people know about your services by contacting your local newspaper to see if there's a story in it for them, print leaflets and distribute them to worthwhile contacts, join a small business group and network like crazy. If you listen to your heart and do things you really want to do then you will automatically have the motivation that will make them happen.

7 **Make changes.** Recognise that as you begin to unlock your inner self you will want to make subtle – or sometimes quite dramatic – changes to the style of clothes you wear, your hair, the colours you choose. Be prepared to embrace these as a true reflection of your authenticity. Bear in mind too, that once a person has the courage to remove their social mask, they frequently wish to discard (or are discarded by) old friends and acquaintances. As your internal environment changes, so too does your external environment in order to support the new you more authentically.

Just be confident that, as less appropriate people move out of your life, new more empowering ones will come in.

Begin to shed your prejudices, your assumptions, your pre-conceptions about how life is or should be (discussed further in Chapter Three). US self-development guru Stephen Covey tells the story of a time when he was travelling on the New York subway and was inconvenienced by a man who got into the car with several children. The youngsters were very noisy and disruptive and, feeling angry and hostile, Covey asked the man if he could try to keep his family under control. The man seemed rather distracted but apologised, saying they had just come from the hospital where his wife – the children's mother – had died that morning. 'I guess they don't know how to handle the situation either,' the man added. In that moment Covey's attitude changed completely to one of sympathy and compassion. Frequently we don't have the full facts upon which we make certain assumptions and judgements about people. Just try to keep an open mind to whatever is going on around you.

8 **Practise being an authentic communicator.** Tell people what you want, how you feel and what is happening with you right now. Too many of us expect our co-workers, partners and friends to have ESP, and put considerable pressure on ourselves and others by bottling up what we really want to say. If you accept that you have the right to be who you are, then you also have a responsibility to ensure that your mind and mouth are operating from the same agenda.

9 **Be good to yourself:** body, mind and spirit. Again, this involves really knowing what turns you on. Don't feel bad about not going down to the gym if exercising leaves you cold. You can be good to your body by taking a regular walk in the countryside, swimming at a health club or by determining to cook yourself the food that you love rather than buying the pre-packaged variety. Buy or borrow the books you have always wanted to read and find the time to lose yourself in them (or the taped versions if you drive a lot and this is more convenient). Stimulate your senses by visiting an art gallery, seeing a show, exploring ancient monuments or stately homes. Give yourself an holistic

boost by treating yourself to a regular day of pampering: either at a salon or at home. Take the phone off the hook once in a while, soak in an aromatherapy bath, pour yourself a glass of your favourite wine, listen to whatever music always stimulates you, rent the video of that film you never got round to seeing in the cinema, or want to see again. Enjoy just pleasing yourself, being with your best friend in all the world: YOU.

~ Affirmations ~

An affirmation is a positive statement that, repeated regularly, helps you change the way you think about yourself. There are a number of guidelines for writing down affirmations, such as writing them in the first person and the present tense.

At the end of each chapter you will find a number of affirmations, relating to the subject just covered, which I recommend you personalise so that they mean something to you: that is, so you *own* them. By outlining the formula for constructing affirmations you will be able to make up your own, very specific statements. Having done that, the rest is up to you: the more frequently you repeat an affirmation the quicker you will change the mind messages you give yourself, and the faster life will follow suit.

Your mind consists of the conscious, of which you are aware, and the subconscious, of which you are not. Neither are willing to be fooled, so if you start saying things like 'I love myself', and it isn't really true, all the negative messages of the past that are stored in your subconscious mind will spring up to contradict you. If you say 'I want to love myself', that will be taken merely as wishful thinking. Alternatively, if you say 'I will love myself', your conscious mind will ask, 'Yes, but when?' Such affirmations are trapped between the present and the future and don't help much either.

The most effective way to construct an affirmation is illustrated by French doctor Emil Coue's original 'cure by autosuggestion'. At the turn of the century he instructed his patients to say: 'Every day in every way I am getting better and better.' By repeating to yourself 'I am becoming more loveable to myself and others', this outlines your positive intention in the present, is realistic and allows you (because we are all human) to slip back from time to time.

Here are eight affirmations you might like to try out before writing some of your own:

- ✔ I am becoming the person I truly want to be.
- ✔ I am resculpting my life into one of happiness and fulfilment.
- ✔ I am learning to accept myself exactly as I am.
- ✔ I am becoming my own best friend.
- ✔ I am taking on the mantle of a spiritual warrior, regarding life's challenges as manageable tasks on my journey towards fulfilment.
- ✔ Every day in every way I am more appreciative of my unique contribution to life.
- ✔ I am starting to recognise that my life has a unique purpose
- ✔ I am moving ever closer to authenticity.

~ Gerry's story ~

The innate skills you demonstrate outside the workplace do have an important part to play in helping you discover work that benefits you and your employer, as illustrated here.

As is the case in many large corporations, Gerry had been promoted far beyond his managerial capabilities. He had been a brilliant technician for the major pharmaceutical company he'd worked for since university, but was considered to be failing spectacularly as a manager.

Gerry was popular within his department. Everybody liked him personally, but he had difficulty delegating, setting clear objectives and keeping track of project deadlines. By the time his company realised what was happening, Gerry had lost much of his technical expertise and was unwilling to lose his status as a manager. Both agreed that early retirement seemed the only solution. However, the company was determined to try one final avenue to retain an otherwise highly valued employee. They brought in Nella Barkley, president of the

Crystal-Barkley Corporation in New York,
design process helps individuals discover and a
skills that are often not recognised as being inv
organisation because they are largely honed out
hours.

During her discussions with Gerry, Nella discovered .
was a leader in his local community. He held a respon.
position on the school board and had devised a number
successful local charity campaigns. Gerry was running for a
seat on the County Council and came across as a very per-
suasive, passionate and articulate man on community issues.
However, he had never mentioned this at work, partly because
he didn't think it was relevant, but mainly because his bosses
might have thought his outside commitments could encroach
on work time.

Nella suggested that Gerry go away and think about why he
was passionate about community issues and the ways in which
he might integrate those motivations into his working life. As
a result, Gerry put forward a proposal that he work as an
advocate for his company with the regulatory authorities. He
joined the Public Affairs division and successfully made many
presentations to various legislative bodies on behalf of the
pharmaceutical industry as a whole. Not only was Gerry happier in his work and enhanced his career as a result, but he
improved the company's standing into the bargain.

✍ Your action list from this chapter

Write down at least six things that you intend to do now – ie, today
not tomorrow – based on what you have learned in this chapter.

1

2

3

4

5

6

CHAPTER THREE

How much do you willingly embrace change?

"Come to the edge," he said.
They said "we are afraid."
"Come to the edge," he said.
They came. He pushed them – and they flew.
Guillaume Apollinaire

For many of us, enforced change is like being made to stand at the edge of an aeroplane door, being bullied into doing a parachute jump. Unwilling to leap out by ourselves we wait and wait until we are pushed by external circumstances – either someone or something – which can result in a much more dramatic and terrifying experience. Not surprising, then, that the phrase 'people hate change' is so deeply embedded in our collective consciousness. Yet the whole of our society is based on the fact that we are changeable. We want to see new movies, wear new fashions, take holidays to places we haven't been before, embrace new experiences and form new relationships. So why do we continue to believe that people are against change?

It is not that change itself is anathema to us, just the fact that we dislike having it imposed on us. For instance, while the majority of us willingly and regularly make changes to our wardrobes to reflect our new taste in clothes, mature adults are unlikely to do so just because a fashion pundit says we must buy this length of skirt or this shape of jacket in order to keep up with current trends. Similarly, we will change, as long as it is in our own time and our expectations of how life is remain in line with how we think it should be. That is why so much of this chapter revolves around the need to change our assumptions about the future, particularly when the main stumbling block stems from regarding the future simply as a variation of the past.

In the same way that our attitudes about ourselves determine how happy and content we are, the conditions, preconceptions and fears we have about the future detrimentally
affect the way we handle changes in our lives. Change has
been defined as a disruption to our expectations. But in many
ways our expectations only appear to be disrupted because we
haven't seen the connection between the different aspects of
our lives.

Take the world of work, for example. The unprecedented
change that is taking place is being driven by the demands of
consumers – that is, each one of us – for products and services
that not only meet our changing needs but suit our ever-
decreasing time frames. Have you noticed how you can get an
immediate answer over the telephone on an application for
credit nowadays? Or the number of products marketed on the
back of offering instant gratification: the meal you can prepare in minutes, the beauty regime that takes no time at all,
the fastest-ever pain relief? Or that delivery services vie for the
quickest turnaround of your parcels and letters? This isn't
simply because a group of marketing managers thought one
day that this might be a good idea, it's because customers
demand it. As our attention-span decreases so does our willingness as consumers to wait for things. In a commercial environment where the difference between product A and B or service C or D hinges not just on the relationship you form with
the person doing the selling, but the speed with which they can
meet your needs, you can begin to appreciate that it is you, in
the guise of consumer, who is driving all this change. And as
the nature of business changes, so too must employers look to
engage people who are flexible, empowered, confident and
passionate enough to capture and maintain customer loyalty
by making quick decisions or taking speedy action.

When we think about organisations' obsession with making
profits for stakeholders, here too each one of us must accept
responsibility. The stakeholders are primarily financial insti-
tutions, such as pensions companies, who are looking for a
good investment on behalf of their beneficiaries: you. But
because this is done institutionally we don't see the link with
ourselves. However, the changing face of employment isn't

happening in a vacuum or because big business wants to make things unpleasant or difficult for us all. It is happening because we, the consumer, are driving it.

There will always be winners and losers in the change game; much depends on how far you can modify your expectations of how life *should* be to how the future *could* be; that is, how well you can adjust your mindset to accepting a certain amount of disruption to your expectations.

The exercises you will find throughout this chapter will not only challenge you to question how far you are embedded in long-held assumptions that inhibit your adaptability, but will help you embrace new paradigms of flexibility. If your list of personal needs in the Introduction (see page 18) put a high priority on working hours, job security, opportunities for promotion and the kind of workplace you feel you work best in, make sure you work through each exercise consistently to help you achieve a more empowering mindset.

~ Jackie's story ~

A complete change of focus – in this case from personal assistant to a director of British Airways to the owner of a company offering balloon décor design – resulted in Jackie expressing a long-held creative passion.

Jackie had worked her way up through the secretarial ranks of British Airways for 12 years, becoming PA to the chief operating officer. When her boss retired, Jackie knew she would have to look for another position within the company or use this opportunity to change direction completely. Aside from her secretarial and IT skills, Jackie had a passion and talent for craftwork. In her spare time she had taken courses on floristry, making wallhangings and designing wedding favours. Through her local country and western club she had successfully produced patterned T-shirts enlivened with glitter, which were in great demand. All these obviously demonstrated Jackie's artistry and talent for intricate design.

It was on a weekend craft course that Jackie was introduced to balloon sculpting and decoration: using these simple devices to create spiral columns, arches and animals for weddings and other special events. On seeing pictures of what could be achieved with just a quantity of coloured balloons, Jackie became fired up in a way she had never done before and wanted to learn everything she could about this new skill. Once she started creating her own balloon arrangements, Jackie found she got an enormous buzz from being on the receiving end of other people's amazement at her talent; what she calls the 'Wow' factor.

While the special-occasion balloon industry is huge in the United States, in Britain it was still burgeoning. With no job forthcoming at British Airways that she was really interested in, Jackie decided to take the plunge, accept the redundancy package they were offering and start herself up in business as Favored Occasions. BA is now one of Jackie's corporate clients and she has arranged balloon sculptures at many business functions, as well as weddings and private parties. While apprehensive about leaving BA because it had been a part of her life for so long, Jackie had fallen in love so much with her balloon work that she was compelled to give it a go. As she explains: 'Life is too short; if there's something you are burning to do, do it. You may have a couple of failures – and I'm expecting that myself – but if you've got the determination to succeed, you'll overcome them.'

With her creativity, imagination and an eye for detail and quality, Jackie is now totally dependent on her business for a regular income. She admits that in the later years of her career with British Airways her heart was no longer in her work and she had resigned herself to never finding her niche in life. All that has changed. Now Jackie advises anyone with a burning passion and creative talent to take that chance, embrace the change and experience what it's like to feel truly fulfilled.

"Life is a series of collisions with the future, it is not the sum of what we have been but what we yearn to be."
Jose Ortega y Gasset

✍ Are you ready to embrace change?

Read the following list of statements and consider whether you agree/disagree with them. Go through the list quickly, circling the first response that comes into your mind.

1 Ideally I would plan my social life ahead of time wherever possible   Agree/Disagree

2 I find it very easy to make snap judgements about people   Agree/Disagree

3 I really enjoy being thrown into situations that I am unfamiliar with   Agree/Disagree

4 I find people who lack spontaneity boring   Agree/Disagree

5 I have a place for everything and everything in its place   Agree/Disagree

6 I feel most secure when people give me clear guidance on how a task should be carried out   Agree/Disagree

7 I listen to and take on board advice before embarking on life-changing decisions   Agree/Disagree

8 I feel most comfortable when I can put routines into my life   Agree/Disagree

9 I get bored easily   Agree/Disagree

10 I don't know how people can cope without words and phrases like 'maybe', 'probably', 'sort of' and 'approximately'   Agree/Disagree

Scoring

Question No	If you agreed	If you disagreed
1 -		Score 1 point
2	Score 2 points	
3	Score 2 points	
4	Score 1 point	
5 -		Score 1 point
6 -		Score 1 point
7 -		Score 2 points
8 -		Score 1 point
9	Score 1 point	
10 -		Score 1 point

Some thoughts and advice about your scores

0–4　You probably enjoy having a fairly well-ordered life and are somewhat averse to risk-taking. You may be open to occasional opportunities to be spontaneous, but probably have a slight resistance to change. You typically take time to weigh up all the pros and cons of any decision, which means that you usually make a sound choice. However, there are occasions in life when opportunities only present themselves for a brief time and sometimes you will need to follow your gut reaction or instinct and 'go for it'. Otherwise you may eventually wonder what you might have achieved; if only you'd left your safety zone a little earlier.

5–8　Generally speaking, you are able to take advantage of opportunities when they arise and also give sufficient thought to embracing challenges when necessary. However, have you thought through whether all the different areas of your life are evenly balanced? Many people who score in this category compartmentalise their lives. For example, at work you may avoid risk and like to be in control of your work environment, but outside of work enjoy having an unpredictable social life filled with highs and lows – or vice versa. The advice in Chapter Eight (Are your work and the rest of your life in balance?) may therefore be of particular relevance to you.

9–13 You face new challenges with enthusiasm and thrive on being thrown into unpredictable situations. People may think of you as impulsive and spontaneous. Some may even admire or be slightly envious of your ability to jump in at the deep end. However, do be aware that while quick decisions are valuable on some occasions, you may benefit from taking a more considered view some of the time. In making life-changing decisions, do you ask for (and listen to) advice from those who care about you? For example, it may seem like a great idea to drop your job for a possibly exciting but loosely defined opportunity, but try to think ahead. What's the impact, not only on yourself but those around you? Even for smaller decisions, do you see things through? Do you sometimes wish that you were more organised?

✎ Exercise: Successfully handling change

To demonstrate that we each cope with change better than we give ourselves credit for, take a look at your Life Line (see page 60). As you glance through it, make a list of the significant changes that have taken place in the past: such as changing jobs where you joined a completely different company; moving to a new area to live; changes in your relationships, particularly long-term ones.

Now recall how you felt about those changes at the time they happened. Were they unnerving and emotionally challenging or uplifting and positive experiences? If you thought any of them were negative at the time, how do you feel about them now? Was that new career the best thing that could have happened to you? Can you now, with hindsight, see the bad side of that long-term relationship and be glad you moved on because you are now with someone who is more loving and caring? Did that house move open your eyes to new possibilities and a chance to experience a fresh perspective?

We can all remember situations when the scenarios we created in our minds were more dramatic and frightening than the reality we actually faced. We just need to remind ourselves of that from time to time.

The real issue here is not so much about managing change, but how we can learn to handle ambiguity. The fact is, we can no longer predict how things will be in the future, based on how they were in the past. That causes us to feel rather unnerved, as we have no experiences on which to fix our innate psychological need for certainty. It's not so much that human beings don't like change, it's that we don't like to feel we are not in control of our lives or, worse still, that events are in the driving seat, not us. This need for control is fed by the conditions, preconceptions and fears we have of ambiguous events, because while change implies we have some sort of idea what to expect, ambiguity is undetermined, vague, obscure, uncertain, equivocal. Therefore what we need are tools and techniques for handling ambiguity rather than change.

In some instances our preconceptions or conditions of how life must be, in order for us to be happy, can inhibit our spiritual growth and development. Sir Benjamin Zander, the conductor of the Boston Philharmonic Orchestra, tells an illuminating story about one of his students who was devastated because his girlfriend of three years had dumped him. Sir Benjamin, in his fatherly role, consoled the youngster but was secretly delighted, recognising that only now would this aspiring musician have the life experience needed to play a particular piece by Schubert – about a young man deserted by his long-time love – with the necessary emotion and empathy.

"Lasting change does not happen overnight.
Lasting change happens in infinitesimal increments
a day, an hour, a minute, a heartbeat at a time."
Sarah Ban Breathnach

✑ Exercise: Challenging assumptions

In today's business world, companies are faced with the fact that yesterday's solutions cannot solve tomorrow's challenges; things are changing too fast for that. Therefore they need to engage in, and surround themselves with people who embody out-of-the-box thinking. Find out to what extent you are locked into assumptions by carrying out the following three exercises.

1 <u>The Nine Dots</u>

Join together all nine dots, using only four straight lines, without taking your pen or pencil off the page at any time or going back over a line. If you have seen this exercise before, and are familiar with the answer, try to think of ways in which you could join all nine dots with just one line.

2 <u>Bill and Hillary</u>
Bill and Hillary are lying dead and naked, in a locked room with a window open. In the middle of the room is an overturned chair surrounded by a pool of water and broken glass. Who are Bill and Hillary and how did they die?

3 <u>Copycats</u>
You are applying for a job where accuracy is extremely important. You are given a notebook where the first sheet of paper is filled with a series of numbers and told to copy these on to the next page exactly. How would you do it? (Note: you cannot use any-thing other than a pen.)

The solutions to these exercises can be found on pages 95–6.

Once you have checked your answers to these posers, think about the assumptions you made in coming to your conclusions. They demonstrate the fact that what we believe is true is simply a set of assumptions relating to the meanings we attribute to events, objects or people, and therefore are not representative of a fixed reality. One of the most empowering ways of journeying through life – yet one of the most difficult for most people – is to think of things not in terms of 'good' or 'bad' but just 'things'. Accept that it is you, through the conditioning you received from your parents or care-givers, education, social influences, etc, who give them their meaning. As one enlightened individual once said: 'There's no such thing as bad weather, just inappropriate clothing.'

Instead of thinking of yourself as vulnerable to the ambiguity that will become an increasing part of our lives as a whole, let alone our working lives, you might try to view life as being full of surprises. After all, most of us are delighted to receive a surprise present from someone, to have a friend ring up out of the blue whom we haven't spoken to for ages, to receive an unexpected bonus, financial or otherwise, at work or to enjoy an unexpected Indian Summer after cooler autumn days have set in. If you can view ambiguity in your working life as simply life throwing you a few surprises once in a while then you will have a much more positive mindset with which to embrace those unexpected circumstances, particularly if you have already established your strengths, talents and passions, and have confidence in your employability.

~ The art of detachment ~

One of the most powerful ways of handling ambiguity is to detach yourself, that is, not to become emotionally tied to specific outcomes. This makes a great deal of sense because whereas you might consider yourself to be the most imaginative person on this planet, the chances are you couldn't dream up in a month of Sundays all the permutations that life, in its benevolence, can offer you.

Many people misinterpret the principle of detachment as meaning we shouldn't have goals or formulate a long-term vision for ourselves. A compelling outcome is vital because it is what we conceive in our minds today that creates and shapes our future. Without a vision we would have a tendency to drift aimlessly through life, not knowing what it is we should be looking for. While you don't want to confuse the map with the territory, if you want to get anywhere without wasting time and resources, it does help to have a map.

However, what is important is to give up the need to have a specific agenda for achieving a particular result. So, while visualising a new career for yourself is a valuable way of testing what it is that engages your heart, and can alert you to possible opportunities that may present themselves in the future, once you have acknowledged that desire you should surrender it to the Universe. I have found this a really helpful mindset to have when chasing jobs or commissions. I simply tell myself that if I am meant to write that book, pen that article, or speak at that conference, then I will; all the chasing up, cajoling, worrying, etc, is simply a waste of my mental and physical energy, which could be put to better use elsewhere.

Again, life presents us with contradictions: the need to take action, to make those calls, to send out your résumé and network like crazy, while simultaneously freeing yourself from the limitations of your past experiences, your preconceptions and assumptions of how things should turn out. Detachment and ambiguity are closely related. The more comfortable you are with what Deepak Chopra terms 'the wisdom of uncertainty', the easier you will find it to detach yourself from a pre-ordained outcome. And in that detachment, ironically, you will find the freedom of possibility: what *could* be rather than what *should* be.

Chopra goes on to say, in *The Seven Spiritual Laws of Success*: 'With uncertainty factored in, you might change direction in any moment if you find a higher ideal, or if you find something more exciting. You are also less likely to force solutions on problems, which enables you to stay alert to opportunities.'

This is particularly important for working from the heart, because when we train our hearts on something – whether a job or a relationship – we have a tendency to believe that nothing else will make us happy or even come along as a substitute. There is nothing wrong in setting your heart on a dream, but it is wise to add a qualifier, as author and self-help expert Susan Jeffers advises. She suggests that you state your specific expectation but then add the words: '... or whatever else the Grand Design has in store for me. It's all happening for my highest good.' If you feel uncomfortable with the words Grand Design, substitute Life, God, the Universe, or a term of your own instead.

Think of your dream vocation in the same way that you would think of your dream partner. While it's all very well to want a tall, dark, attractive, romantic, passionate, articulate and reasonably well-off partner to share your life with, once you start dictating that they should be a certain height, a doctor or a lawyer, own a city apartment and a country mansion, be unmarried with no children cluttering up the past – and refuse to look at anyone who doesn't fit these precise specifications – you can see how easy it would be to spend the rest of your life alone.

There is in fact a scientific basis for the spiritual law of detachment which comes from the fascinating work being done by Doctors Robert G Jahn and Brenda Dunne of the Princeton Engineering Anomalies Research division at Princeton University in the United States. While undertaking a rigorous scientific study of human consciousness, the PEAR team asked volunteers to consciously attempt to influence random number generators, using the power of their minds. It appeared that those individuals who made up their minds to influence the machine but then engaged in no further mental effort – that is, they thought of what they wanted to achieve, then detached from the outcome and just let it happen – were the most successful in this experiment. As Dr Dunne explained: 'If they try harder and harder they become frustrated and the effect remains elusive. If they just let it happen, relax, have fun and gently encourage and tease the machine into co-operating, the effect returns and is often even more pronounced.'

"He who predicts the future lies,
even if he tells the truth."
Old Arab proverb

~ Secrets of high-performing companies ~

Re-inventing themselves is not just something movie and pop stars do; major organisations have also realised that to succeed – indeed, survive – in today's ever-changing, fickle marketplace, they need to take on board a flexible approach – not just in attitude, but even in terms of how they categorise their businesses. Traditional barriers between industries are collapsing and it is becoming increasingly difficult to point to any company and say categorically that they are in car manufacturing, financial services, or food retailing. Major supermarket chains, such as Tesco in Britain, now own banks, petrol stations and are becoming internet providers. The Finnish company Nokia, once a paper-making business, is now a leading manufacturer of mobile phones. Car-makers such as Toyota and General Motors are dipping their toes into the satellite broadcasting market. Utility companies have stopped thinking of themselves purely as being in electricity, gas, or oil, and see themselves as energy providers. Arguably, one of the biggest names to have successfully broadened its appeal, originally known as an airline and music company, is Richard Branson's Virgin Group, which now embraces Virgin cola, condoms, cinemas, financial services and trains.

When the chairman of Revlon called his sales force together to ask them what business they thought they were in, the team predictably replied, 'selling cosmetics'. Charles Revson corrected them, saying: 'No. We're in the business of selling dreams.' Which, let's face it, offers much wider potential than flogging a range of eyeshadows or foundations.

Think of some of the most successful brand names in the world today and look at the bigger picture: what that brand means to the consumer other than the products it sells. Brands such as Ferrari and Marlboro which, through their links with motor racing, now mean excitement and not just cars and cigarettes, allowing them to successfully expand into selling fragrances and clothing. And Lucozade, originally developed as a glucose drink for invalids and convalescents, has repositioned itself as an energy provider to trendy sports enthusiasts and now offers a wide variety of flavoured drinks as well as tablets.

✍ Exercise: Developing your 'Brand Identity'

There is a lot that individuals can learn from the way that organisations position themselves in the marketplace; namely that handling change becomes easier when you take a broader view of your working life. Start by imagining yourself as a brand. Firstly, think of all the core values – the moral principles or standards – that you embody. If you are unclear about your values, asking yourself the following questions should help you uncover them:

● What's important to you about what you do? For example, is it vital for you to always be honest in your interactions with others, to gain experience at any cost, to be seen as unique or different?

● What standards do you live by: ie, what would you not do or sacrifice for anything?

● What matters most to you in life? Is your integrity and professional reputation more important to you than any amount of money, for example?

● Who or what would you lay down your life for? You may not have thought of yourself as family oriented because you devote so much of your time to your work but, when push comes to shove, would you give everything up to save your child's or partner's life?

● What traits do you admire in others? Their 'can-doism', self-motivation, open-mindedness, etc?

● What intrinsic self-worth do you set great store by?

● What wouldn't you change, even if it put you at a disadvantage?

Try not to get locked into what core values are socially acceptable, for example believing that you should want to put your family above your work. Consider also whether any parts of your list are in conflict with any others, such as wanting the freedom to engage in the work you love while needing to be emotionally tied to a co-dependent relationship.

Once you have a list of values, write these into these three concentric circles, with the most important ones at the centre. For example, your values circle might look like this:

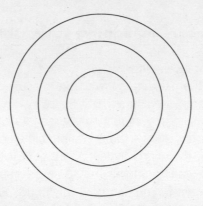

<u>Inner circle</u>: Compassionate, open, honest, integrated, spiritually aware, reputable, aspirational.
<u>Middle circle</u>: Loyal, unique, inquisitive, approachable, open-minded, motivating, balanced.
<u>Outer circle</u>: Inspiring, appreciative, altruistic, confident, generous.

Put into your circle as many values as you consider to be truthful and relevant, with the most important ones in the centre, and the others radiating out.

Now, developing this idea of yourself as a brand entity, draw a triangle, and insert the appropriate headings. Then fill in each of the boxes with a couple of sentences that say something about you in relation to those subjects. The following notes may help you.

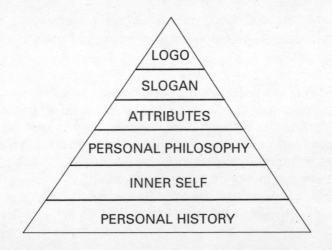

Personal History: What is there particularly about your background and experience that has contributed to your uniqueness? Try to sum this up in as few words as possible. One way to do this is to copy the way in which film scriptwriters have to reduce their storylines to a short sentence in order to sell them to Hollywood studios. My favourite is the following description of the 1970s film *Love Story*, starring Ali McGraw and Ryan O'Neal: 'Two students fall in love; she dies.' How can you encapsulate your life history into just a few words?

Inner Self: Look back at the exercises and notes you made in Chapter Two (pages 55–61). What do they reveal about who you really are? To help you get a handle on this essence in a more visual or tangible way, is there a famous character, fictional or real, who best represents the essential you? For example, if you consider yourself to be someone in charge of his/her life, who doesn't feel the need to apologise for personal choices, who is energising and not afraid to take risks, someone who is non-threatening to both men and women, perhaps you might personify yourself as the actress Sharon Stone?

Personal Philosophy: What underpins your beliefs, your values, and your behaviours? If you had to come up with one phrase that highlights these, what would it be? Mine is: 'Everything is unfolding as it should and will ultimately be for my highest good'. You might find that an age-old proverb (a list of which can be found in any good dictionary of quotations) best identifies your own philosophy on life. For example, 'Do as you would be done by' or 'Knowledge is power' or 'Doing is better than saying'.

Attributes: What are your particular skills and competencies? Look beyond job-related or academic qualifications to qualities and virtues such as being a good listener, a loyal friend, someone who sticks it out when the going gets tough, a person with whom strangers instantly feel comfortable, or someone who gains others' trust easily.

Finally, in terms of your brand identity, how would you advertise yourself? What logo or advertising slogan would you use? Can you think of a catchy one-liner that – if you were a product – would identify what you are about and allow you to sell yourself successfully to customers?

The purpose of this exercise within this chapter is to help you think 'out of the box' and to broaden the way you perceive yourself. In today's world of work we must all think of ourselves as flexible 'brands' so that, as needs and demands change, we can adapt and reposition ourselves to be continually compelling and relevant to our internal and external customers: our employers, suppliers and co-workers. In Chapter Four (What do you really want to do?) we will develop this theme further in order to uncover the work that engages your heart and which you love to do – so keep your notes in a safe place.

~ Your choice ~

One of the key messages of this book is that there is always more than one way of interpreting things. When you choose to view circumstances or people in a particular way you are exercising control, which may make you feel more comfortable in the short term, but which can eventually result in attitudes that are limiting and dysfunctional. Which of the following lists do you currently respond to? In what ways can you enhance your life by changing your mind to the more positive perspective?

I choose to be:

trusting	controlling
involved	insular
powerful	weak
bold	frightened
joyful	sad
forgiving	resentful
content	dissatisfied
complete	empty
in the present moment	shackled by the past
creative	unimaginative
confident	doubtful
resilient	vulnerable
loving	needy
excited	tranquillised.

Assumptions about
~ redundancy and unemployment ~

The likelihood is that at some time in our lives we are each going to hear the words: 'Sorry, but we're going to have to let you go.' Even the self-employed aren't exempt from periods when there may be no work in the order book and you begin to wonder how you are going to survive, not just economically but psychologically. It is periods like these that test us to the limit and why it is so essential to know ourselves well enough to be able to tap into our inner reserves of trust, self-confidence and a belief in life having a meaning.

Feelings of rejection can swamp you at this time, producing emotional extremes ranging from anger and fear to grief and guilt. But rejection in the form of losing your job is only shameful and humiliating if you choose to see it that way. Many people have chosen to view unemployment as a time to 'mentally re-group', to tune into what their hearts have been telling them, not just their minds. To reflect not just on their skills and experience but on the attitudes that may be preventing them from developing themselves fully and creatively. Most of the people to whom I have spoken have said they now look back at their redundancy and see that it was the best thing that could have happened to them, because it forced them to make changes that they were otherwise too fearful or hesitant to make by themselves.

Unfortunately, society sets great store only on paid employment, which is why the work of homemakers and voluntary workers is so seriously undervalued, and some women in particular perpetuate this with comments like: 'I'm just a housewife.' But there is no compulsion for you to get tied into that way of thinking. Organisations are slowly beginning to recognise that skills and experience honed outside the workplace can have a valuable part to play within it, which is why some corporate initiatives exist to help employees engage in non-vocational and personal development learning. There is no differentiation made between learning that adds to the job and that which adds to personal context and family life, because even learning for its own sake has a knock-on benefit for the business by enhancing employees' self-confidence and self-image.

While you would have to be a saint – or at least a highly enlightened individual – not to be knocked back by a period of unemployment or enforced redundancy, it is true to say that the more faith you have in your employability, and the more trust you place that life and the lessons it teaches us will lead us towards even greater emotional and spiritual fulfilment, then the easier it will be to pick up the pieces when crises do happen. But sometimes good old pragmatism is what's called for. Let's look again at the list of why we work, outlined in Chapter One. Work offers us:

- a structure to our lives
- varied, enforced activity
- social contact
- job satisfaction
- a sense of importance
- financial security
- avoidance of relationship and other issues
- status
- certainty
- a sense of belonging.

Now let's use that list – as well as other advice – to prepare for possible periods of unemployment in the future.

~ Surviving job loss ~

1 If you are the sort of person who is more comfortable with a sense of structure to your life, then build one, as a safety net, that has nothing to do with your job. Engage in activities that use the amount of available time you have while employed but could be expanded upon during periods of unemployment. For example, you may have some connection with a local charity or community group which would not only engage you to a greater extent if you had the time, but may have some bearing on a new direction of 'heart work'. This type of work would also take care of the need for varied, enforced activity, social contact, job satisfaction, a sense of importance and a sense of belonging.

2 If you want to ensure you are financially secure enough
   to weather periods of enforced unemployment, what are
   you doing now to make that happen? To help you see
   where savings could be made, check out the advice in
   Chapter Five (Do you work purely for the money?).

3 Sadly, neither workaholism nor presenteeism (the concept
   of staying long hours at work to show commitment, even
   though there is little or nothing for you to do) will
   guarantee you job security nowadays. If you are using
   your job as a shield in order to avoid facing problems in
   your relationships, your lack of a social life, or to give
   you no time in which you might have to face yourself,
   then when that job disappears you will be at an even
   greater disadvantage, as outlined in Chapter Eight (Are
   your work and the rest of your life in balance?). Take
   courage and face whatever it is you are afraid of confronting – and stop using your work as a crutch.

4 The status we get from a job is an ephemeral thing. The
   reason why so many senior executives go into major
   decline after retiring – and sometimes die very quickly of
   a heart attack – is because they can no longer cope with
   losing the adulation and respect that had come with their
   position, as well as saying goodbye to the company car
   and expense account. This is another example of the value
   of living a balanced life, one that won't go pear-shaped
   when one aspect of it disappears, temporarily or
   permanently. Many of the corporate leaders interviewed
   by Dr Harry Alder for his book *Think Like a Leader*
   make time for interests such as running marathons, fly
   fishing, gardening or various sports. Leisure activities can
   give you a sense of achievement far greater than the
   transient status from material possessions or outside
   approbation, as can a greater degree of introspection.
   When people are faced with a life-threatening condition,
   lose a partner or experience a close family member dying,
   they quickly realise the extent to which we all put too
   much emphasis on the external things in life. We can
   learn from their experiences by concentrating now on
   what is really important: things like our health and the
   love of the people around us. Externally enhanced status

is irrelevant because it is not who we are. Remember, the
only respect you need is self-respect.

5 Take this free time to think about who you really want to
   be, what you truly want to do with your life, and then
   plan it, step by step. Use this opportunity to engage in
   the exercises in this book and to read other personal
   development titles in a deeper, more leisurely way than is
   possible when you are holding down a full-time job.
   Then, after being truthful with yourself, investigate what
   it is you need to do in terms of self-development and
   skills acquisition to relaunch yourself in a working
   environment. Remember, long periods of introspection
   are hard to come by for the majority of employed people.
   Unemployment is sometimes the only way to stop and
   re-evaluate your life.

6 Avoid the knee-jerk reaction of accepting the first thing
   that's offered to you. Take the opportunity to change
   yourself and, in doing so, change the high-risk situation
   you are in. Once you have found your vocation – only
   achieved by listening, waiting and trusting – you will
   become so employable that you will never again fear
   those words, 'I'm afraid we're having to let you go.'

Faith in your future is essential at times of greatest challenge.
Which is why visualisation is such a useful tool. Companies
call it 'scenario planning'. Unable to predict precisely what the
future holds, yet needing to make decisions today to prepare
themselves for future demands, they fantasise about a number
of possible future scenarios: looking first at the wider picture
and then focusing in on the details. Which, given the age-old
spiritual and philosophical belief that we each construct our
futures by our present thoughts and actions, makes absolute
sense.

Scenario planning was pioneered by companies like Royal
Dutch/Shell in the early 1970s when a number of crises
throughout the oil industry revealed huge cracks in the way
companies went about corporate forecasting. What emerged
was a dramatically different way that businesses could gear
themselves up to face the future. Scenario planning doesn't
just deal with the business of facts and statistics, but with

people's perceptions. It involves 'thinking the unthinkable' as one UK government minister was recently assigned to do; to mentally prepare for the unpredictable. Whereas old-fashioned forecasting focuses on certainties (which are increasingly rare in today's ever-changing world) and the misguided assumption that the future can be predicted by looking at what happened in the past, scenario planning asks, 'What if?' and 'Why not?': both hallmarks of successful and creative individuals.

Take some quiet time, by yourself, to fantasise about your future. Visualisations are most effective when they engage all the senses, so in your mind's eye make the experience as vivid as possible: see your future; smell, taste, feel, hear and 'know' what it will be like. Make a note of any emotions that rise up at this time. Listen to your heart as well as your head and be aware of any scenarios that you are drawn to simply because they offer you the greatest security or the most money. Then, when you have formulated a compelling future for yourself, think of an alternative; perhaps keeping some of the most essential aspects of the first scenario but with adaptations in certain areas, such as where you might be living, the exact nature of the job you will be doing, etc. When you have completed that scenario, think of another – and another. Don't restrict yourself until you have come up with four to six different scenarios for working from the heart in the future. Then, and only then, should you start to work backwards and look at the actions and attitudes you will need to change today to bring them to fulfilment.

If it would help to write this down rather than formulate it in your head, turn to the letter exercise in Chapter Nine (page 185). Finally, don't forget to disengage your emotions from expecting a specific outcome. Let it go.

---

*"Man does not simply exist but always decides
what his existence will be,
what he will become in the next moment.
By the same token, every human being has the
freedom to change at any moment."
Viktor Frankl*

✎ Exercise: Changing your internal dialogue

Listening to the language people use, particularly when talking about their problems, is a fascinating exercise. Before you examine your own linguistic filters, do some active listening today with a friend, your partner, or a relative. Ask them questions like, 'What do you want from a job?' or 'What's important about what you do for a living?', and make a note of the words they use to answer.

People who are motivated away from something will tell you what they don't want, such as: 'I don't want to be rigidly working nine to five'; 'I don't want anything that means working long hours or travelling away from my family.' These people are motivated by negatives and threats. They are likely to be the ones who will stick something out until it becomes so unbearable that they are forced to make changes to their work or lifestyle. The problem is, because 'away from' people are so fixated on what they don't want, they often repeat mistakes in careers and relationships because they don't actually know what to replace the status quo with.

Individuals who are oriented to moving towards something have their sights clearly focused on their goals. Their language will describe clearly what it is they are looking for, such as, 'Personal relationships are important to me so I look for co-workers who are friendly, open and I feel I can get on with' or 'I need to feel that I am creating value; that I'm making a difference in what I do for a living.'

Once you can clearly recognise the difference between 'away from' and 'moving towards' motivations, listen – by taping yourself or asking a friend to jot down some key phrases – to your own dialogue. In the same way that you can change your mind any time you like, you can change the language you use. And becoming more positive in your speech patterns, by focusing on what you want rather than what you don't want, can help you make change more palatable because you allow yourself to see the benefits of what lies ahead, not just the relief of extricating yourself from an unpleasant situation.

~ Family support ~

Always remember that changes in your life will have an impact on those around you. While you are focused on dealing with ambiguity, or becoming excited at the prospect of actively changing your world to fulfil long-held dreams, your partner, children, family and, to a lesser extent, your friends may find this threatening. During any period of potential and actual change it is vital to encourage open and free discussion between everyone concerned. Talk to your loved ones about your plans, ask their opinions: how do they feel about your ideas? Can they envisage any pitfalls, anything you could do that would make the path smoother? Test out some scenario planning with them and make sure that their lives are taken into account when you come to look at the finer details.

For example, if your dream involves selling up and moving to rural France to start a wine-distribution business, how will that affect your partner's job, your children's education, your elderly parents who rely on you? While I am not saying that you should get too bogged down in pragmatics and end up having to shelve your plans, it is sensible to take relevant parties through all the steps you plan to go through so that you don't give them a huge shock when you suddenly announce that you are jacking in your City job to become a potter in the country. All change is personal, but that doesn't mean to say that it is confined to just you.

The biggest danger we all face when handling ambiguity is not failure, it is irrelevancy. In this new era of perpetual unrest, you can choose whether to be a victim or a revolutionary, and to view life's challenges as the tasks of a spiritual warrior or a fall guy. Now that we have dealt with who you are and the extent to which you can become a chameleon in order to survive in an ever-changing world, we are going to link that with your innate skills, talents and passions in order to determine what it is you really want to do for a living: the kind of work you will love because it fully reflects YOU.

AFFIRMATIONS

✔ I am preparing myself to embrace and benefit from the change and ambiguity in my life.

✔ I am becoming more and more comfortable with uncertainty.

✔ I am actively changing the language I use to express what I want out of life.

✔ I am choosing to release the fear that ties me to a life I no longer desire.

✔ I am becoming more aware of the assumptions and preconceptions I have that stop me moving forwards.

✔ I am committed to dreaming my ideal futures, taking the necessary actions to help bring them to reality, and then detaching from being emotionally tied to a specific outcome.

✔ I am becoming flexible enough to change direction or seize new opportunities that best represent the unique individual I am.

✔ Every day in every way I am working towards becoming more employable and hence more secure in my working life.

✒ Your action list from this chapter

Write down at least six things that you intend to do now – ie, today not tomorrow – based on what you have learned in this chapter.

1

2

3

4

5

6

✍ Solutions to the assumption exercises

1 The Nine Dots

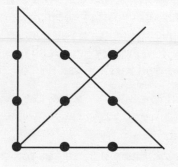

There are several ways to solve this puzzle, but this is the most common. For the 'one-line only' answers you could have suggested using a marker pen with a nib so thick that it covered all nine dots in one stroke; or to paste the nine dots pattern on to a ball or globe and then draw a single circular line around it until they were all joined. Alternatively, you could have tried scrunching the paper with nine dots drawn on into a ball and then poking a pen through it to join them into one.

Most people fail this exercise because they keep their pen or pencil within the box rather than believe they can go outside it. We confine ourselves to unspoken rules all the time. Think about how often you restrict yourself when you should be thinking 'out of the box'.

2 Bill and Hillary
Bill and Hillary are goldfish who died when their bowl of water (hence the broken glass and fluid on the floor) was knocked off the stool by a strong gust of wind through the open window. Did the names of the US President and his wife cause you to think that these were human beings? Did the word naked also lead you to assume that they were people? To what extent do you take minimal information and create an entire, and largely inaccurate, scenario around it?

3 Copycats

The applicants who actually got the job in the City bank that devised this 'test' were the ones who ripped out the first sheet and, holding it alongside the second page, could most easily – and hence accurately – copy the figures.

Did the fact that this exercise was concerned with accuracy and numbers cause your logical left rather than your creative right brain to muddy the solution? Again, do you confine yourself to self-imposed rules – such as not ripping out sheets from a book – even though no one has said that you can't?

"He who has a why to live for
can bear with almost any how."
Nietzsche

CHAPTER FOUR

What do you really want to do?

*"Everyone has his own specific vocation or mission in life
to carry out a concrete assignment which demands fulfilment.
Therein he cannot be replaced, nor can his life be repeated."*
Victor Frankl

Have you ever wondered why some pop and film stars, who are thrust into the limelight and earn vast sums of money as well as the adulation of millions, descend into a lifestyle of drink, drugs and one dysfunctional relationship after another, while others cope perfectly well with their fame? Could it be that the former have grasped at a chance of wealth, power and material trappings at the expense of their authentic selves? As was discussed in Chapter Two, anyone who is trying to mask an inner insecurity, shyness, inferiority complex, or low self-esteem by pretending to be someone they are not – and remember that film stars have public personas aside from the celluloid roles they play – puts an unbearable strain on their Inner Self. Whereas someone who really is a natural extrovert, 'show off', egotist, drama queen or whatever, is in a much better position to enjoy a glamorous and famous lifestyle because their 'work' allows them simply to be themselves.

Similarly, you will only find true contentment at work when it is an extension of who you really are. Which is why it is so important to excavate the Inner You before trying to discover and articulate what you want to do for a living.

This chapter pulls together the discoveries you have made about yourself in some of the earlier exercises and links them with a further exploration of your values, interests, motivations, life skills and heart's desire. Unlike many career-focused inventories and advice, this book encourages you to recognise that *capability* is not the same as *suitability*. You may have consummate shorthand and typing skills, but if in your heart you dream of running your own country tea shop then you are never going to be a truly happy or committed secretary or

PA. Your job-related skills may help you earn a living but they won't always assist you to fulfil your life.

~ Work as a mission ~

One of the most profound and perplexing questions we can ask ourselves is: 'Why am I here?' Finding your mission in life, the unique purpose for which you exist on this planet (and although at times you may feel sceptical of this, you do have one), answers that question and enriches your life with a greater sense of meaning. The starting point for finding your unique mission – the spiritual route map against which everything you do in your life is measured – involves looking at yourself from the inside out.

In the materialistic 'me first' world of our personalities or Egos, we are programmed to expect our own needs to be met, and we make that goal paramount. In the altruistic reality of the soul it is service to others that is so inspiring (a word, incidentally, that comes from the same Latin word as spirit: *spiritus,* meaning to breathe or give life). When we work from the heart we tap into the desire to make a difference to other people's lives through what we produce, how we interact with others, how we *are*. And strangely enough, by meeting the needs of others we often find our own needs are met more readily.

All we have to do is to commit to living with passion, to choose work that is consistent, not just with our skills and talents, but with our values; to remember that we are human *beings* not human *doings*. It is the difference between being a nurse and being a nurse who every day demonstrates care, compassion and love for patients; it is the difference between working in a team and working to support, empower and coach each member of that team to be the very best they can be. It is the difference between producing a piece of art that is technically brilliant and will earn you a lot of money and producing a piece of art that reaches out and touches the soul of every onlooker, reader or listener, and in so doing fills them with positive energy.

None of this is as rare as it may seem. Every day people are doing ordinary jobs in an extraordinary way. Such as the concierge who believes his job is to ensure visitors to 'his' hotel (note the ownership) have the most enjoyable stay and is proud of his part in helping them achieve that. Or the photographer who doesn't just take photographs but says her job is to capture the essential beauty – the soul – of every one of her subjects, regardless of their physical appearance. Or the factory worker who doesn't just believe he puts the wheel nuts on family cars but prides himself on making each car safe for families to drive in. Or the labourer who doesn't just think of himself as carrying hods of bricks but says he is helping to build someone a beautiful home.

In the film *You've Got Mail*, Meg Ryan's character sums up the whole notion of a 'personal signature' when she says that her mother, who had run a wonderful children's bookstore in New York, didn't just sell books but helped children become the people they were meant to be by introducing them to inspiring literature.

These personal signatures are evident everywhere and you only have to change your attitude to work to create your own. By engaging your heart in your work today and recognising the bigger picture of what you do – regardless of whether it is the ideal job for you or not – you will not only enhance other people's lives but achieve greater personal satisfaction into the bargain.

Finding the work you love:
~ constructing the Heartwork Plan ~

Unlike most other books on finding the right career path, *Working from the Heart* ignores the 'how', and concentrates first on the 'why' and then the 'what' of your life's mission. This is because when you have found a vocation that resonates with you, the 'how' seems to take care of itself. That's not to say you don't have to take some action by ensuring you have the right skills for the work you are drawn to and then identifying the best environment in which to express yourself. But it is remarkable how life, once you have made the first mental connection, assists by bringing you into contact with just the right people, at the right time, in the right way. One of the biggest clues life offers you as to whether or not your vocational choice is true 'heart work' is the number of serendipitous events that bring you nearer to your goals.

However, it's worth pointing out here that this is not meant to be a definitive guidebook to a specific job. It is not the purpose of this book – nor is it possible to do this without having the opportunity to analyse your answers to the exercises you have completed – to suggest you should go away and be a car mechanic, start your own desktop-publishing business, or sell children's party cakes. The Heartwork Plan you will end up with is not a skills inventory but a mirror of who you truly are so that you can then intuitively choose work that is an accurate reflection of that. What this Plan will do is provide you with the tools for further research so that you can then investigate different vocational or career paths to fit your inner needs. In short, this book will help you find the essence of the work you desire, not the form. It is then up to you to find the best fit between you and a completely new avenue of expression, or one that is a refinement of what you currently do for a living.

"People tend to confuse their purpose (What do I love to do?) with their ideals (How am I comfortable behaving?) and their desired results (What can I achieve?). If you untangle those questions, and compare the answers with your natural talents and abilities, you'll start down the path to success."
Robin Hirschberg, founder,
Not So New Age Consulting

✍ Exercise: Constructing your Heartwork Plan

Because this is the most interactive chapter in this book, make
sure you have read and completed the previous exercises before
going any further. To benefit most from the advice outlined in this
chapter, try to allow at least a day of 'me' time to prepare and
then reflect on your Heartwork Plan. For this you will need:

1　Your Life Line notes (see pages 60–61) together with eight to
　 ten examples of 'top line' happy and successful situations in
　 your life when you experienced a feeling of connection and
　 fulfilment, regardless of your age, the activity or the environ-
　 ment you were in. In addition, pull out several examples of
　 negative occasions that represent major issues in your life,
　 such as dealing with your parent's divorce, a failed marriage, a
　 period of unemployment, etc.
2　Your list of personal needs (see page 18): the priority you put
　 on what's important to you. Take the opportunity to look at
　 your list again and change it where it feels right to do so.
3　Your Values Circle (see page 84): the moral principles or
　 standards that you embody and their order of importance
　 to you.
4　Your Brand Identity triangle (see page 84), which depicts you
　 in a wider context than the job or career path you may have
　 got locked into.

You will also need to buy an A1 sheet of thin card. Stationery or
art shops usually have a wide selection for just a few pounds.
Draw on this card an enlarged copy of the chart illustrated on
page 102, leaving plenty of space around each section for your
notes. Having everything on one large sheet of paper will more
easily help you see the links between all the different areas of
self-exploration.

　Don't fill in your chart until you have reached the end of this
chapter – if not the end of the book – as we still have more
exploring to do, starting with the next topic.

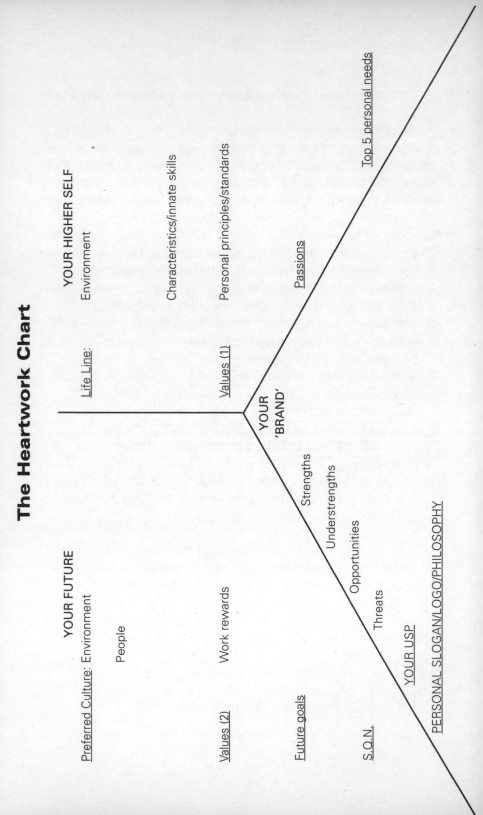

The Heartwork Chart

YOUR HIGHER SELF

Life Line:

Environment

Characteristics/innate skills

Values (1)

Personal principles/standards

Passions

Top 5 personal needs

YOUR 'BRAND'

Strengths

Understrengths

Opportunities

Threats

YOUR USP

PERSONAL SLOGAN/LOGO/PHILOSOPHY

YOUR FUTURE

Preferred Culture: Environment

People

Work rewards

Values (2)

Future goals

S.Q.N.

✍ Exercise: Your future goals

© Nicholson McBride

Below is a list of ten personal goals that relate to your life as a whole. Think of your future and what you would like to have in it. Rank these ten life goals in terms of what you would like to achieve in the future, with the most important as 1 and 10 for the least important. Questions you might wish to ask yourself before beginning this task include:

- Do you like to serve or be served?
- Do you prefer to lead or be led?
- Is earning lots of money more important to you than spending time with your friends or family?
- What is more important to you, independence and freedom or the security offered by your family?

By taking each of these ten goals and checking them against the other nine, you will achieve a hierarchy that accurately reflects the order in which each of these is important to you. There may well be trade-offs that you will have to make in any future work and this will highlight your priorities for you.

No judgement is implied in any of these questions and you should try not to judge yourself when answering them. To be truly authentic involves being who you are, not what other people expect you to be, or what is considered socially acceptable. You will achieve much more out of these exercises if you are truthful about yourself.

Leadership: To become an influential leader or manager; to organise, coach or assist others to achieve community or organisational goals.
Expertise: To become an authority on a special subject; to persevere in learning to become an expert in a particular skill or accomplishment.
Prestige: To achieve recognition, awards or high social status. To become well known for whatever you do.
Service: To be helpful to others and contribute to their satisfaction and needs.

Wealth: To earn lots of money and be in a position of owning material possessions that attract you.

Independence: To have the freedom to do whatever you like, including being your own boss at work. Not to have any ties that impinge on that freedom.

Affection: To have the companionship and affection of family and friends.

Self-realisation: To realise your full creative potential and be totally happy/at peace with yourself.

Pleasure: To enjoy life and to have an abundance of what is important to you.

Now spend some time thinking about your top five goals and ask yourself why these are important to you. Consider the following questions:

Leadership: What personal and professional skills do you need to develop to make you a more effective leader? To what extent are you prepared to spend time and even money doing this? Is your heart truly into leadership as a form of service (the mark of a great leader) or to mask feelings of inadequacy?

Expertise: Why do you want to be seen as an expert? Because you are passionate about it or because it will earn you more money? Is the subject you have chosen one where you bring a part of yourself to the equation (ie, a subjective choice) or is it purely an intellectual exercise?

Prestige: What is it exactly that you want to achieve and why is this important to you? Do you see prestige and power as linked?

Service: How do you define service and how will you know when you have achieved it? What is it that you get out of serving others? Do you confuse service with sacrifice (as in 'I'll help you because I feel guilty about something.')?

Wealth: Do you confuse money with happiness? What is it about being wealthy that is important to you?

Independence: To what extent are you truly self-sufficient? Do you expect others to support you emotionally or financially while believing you live an independent existence?

Affection: Is your working life making it easy for you to be a good companion to your loved ones? Is there a balance in your life between your being affectionate and caring to others and getting this back? To what extent do you give out affection and expect to receive it in equal measures?

Self-realisation: What does being creative mean to you? How will you know when you are happy? What circumstances will contribute to this for you?

Pleasure: What constitutes pleasure for you? How will you know when you have achieved this state? To what extent are you able to achieve pleasure for yourself or are you looking for external circumstances to provide it for you?

Remember, as with all these self-assessment exercises there is no right or wrong answer, they are merely a springboard to understanding what motivates you, and to help you achieve a balance between external and internal needs. When you are satisfied with the order of your top five goals, write them in the appropriate section on your Heartwork Plan.

    Now let's start filling in the rest of the Plan, beginning with the right-hand segment – Your Higher Self.

✎ Exercise: Heartwork Plan: Your Higher Self

Life Line achievements and issues
Look at the notes you produced from the Life Line exercise in Chapter Two (pages 60–61). These contain a lot of invaluable information, not just about what satisfiers and drivers – ie, external factors – you need to put in place in order to be at your happiest, but also the achievements and characteristics that you tell you – and therefore any future employer – what you are good at.

Satisfiers and drivers
From the selection of eight to ten 'top line' life experiences you have chosen, analyse what it was that encouraged a sense of fulfilment or flow in those instances.

- What factors are common to all these experiences? Perhaps it was having a variety of physical tasks to do, or intellectual challenges; perhaps it was being involved with helping others, or working independently?
- Was it being with a particular kind of person that made the difference for you, or a particular environment?

- What was it that emotionally underpinned those experiences? Try to tap into the feelings you had at the time. Part of the journey towards finding your heart's work is knowing what you want, but an equally valuable part involves knowing what you will feel like when you get it.
- What aspect of your Inner Self did you bring to each of these experiences that moved you or brought you joy?

Once you have identified as many common motivational factors as possible from these past experiences, jot them down in the relevant section of your Heartwork Plan.

Characteristics/innate skills
Now let's look at examples where you faced particular negative challenges in your life. Jot down briefly on a sheet of paper what these were – at least six if possible – then, alongside each highlight what inner reserves you drew on to overcome those issues.

For example, your parents' divorce may have led you to become independent at an early age; to accept uncertainty in life and hence be better able to handle change; to analyse what went wrong in their relationship so you made informed choices in your relationships.

For each life issue, try to uncover four to six characteristics that represent a positive outcome of that negative experience. With six different issues you may end up with 24 to 36 adjectives, many of which are repetitions or synonyms. Hone this list down to six or eight innate factors that you have brought to bear when faced with major challenges in your life, and write these on your Heartwork Plan.

Values
In the preceding chapters we have looked at two different kinds of values: those expectations or guiding principles that make a difference or are seen as important to you. In the Introduction (What is important to you?) and in this chapter (Your future goals, pages 103–5) you looked at a number of work-related rewards, such as prestige, finances, influence and power, professional growth and learning, etc.

Now compare these two lists, your hierarchy of personal needs from page 18 and your top five goals from page 103. You should see some cross-over that highlights your external motivators. These give you a handle on the rewards you value when considering various vocational options, and the priority you put on each.

In Chapter Three (page 84) you were encouraged to draw your Values Circle containing those internal values that represent, for you, the 'right way' to do things. Both of these lists – your inner circle values and the top five work-related goals – will need to be met by anyone you are considering working with or for – otherwise you will be faced with values conflicts.

Before writing your values into your Heartwork Plan, however, take some time to consider whether they reflect the real you or whether they are expectations you have absorbed from your parents or society in general. Make sure that these are values you have chosen to live your life by, and not had imposed on you by others.

~ Avoiding values conflicts ~

A combination of our scarcity mentality when it comes to jobs, and also the fact that the formality of job applications and interviews tends to unnerve the majority of us, means we frequently overlook the need to check whether a company's values are consistent with our own. Instead of trying to fit the mould of how somebody else wants you to be, look upon this process as a two-way street. You will be happier and more successful if you are yourself in any work that you do, and because of that your effectiveness will be enhanced: a win:win situation for both you and your employer. If the company you think you want to work for is very people focused and has put in place lots of team building, peer coaching and customer-service initiatives, there will be little benefit to you or to them if you are someone who likes to work independently with little or no human contact.

Try not to wear rose-coloured spectacles and believe everything will be all right once you're working somewhere. I remember being desperate to get a job in television after completing my secretarial training with the BBC. The course assessors had rather astutely found me a job in the publicity department, but I wanted to work in programming, and as soon as I could I started applying for other jobs.

I was invited along to an interview for a job as a production secretary on a programme in the TV current affairs department and was given the opportunity to chat to the two existing production secretaries who had been there some time. They both advised me to turn the offer down should I get it, explaining that there wasn't enough work for the two of them as it was and that their supervisor was a dreadful woman who put the fear of God into everybody. Did I listen? Not a chance. I was fixated on getting a job in television – any job – if it killed me. So I spent the next year, after accepting their offer, miserably kicking my heels and being bullied by the harridan from hell. I had decided my colleagues were mistaken or were trying to stop me having as good a job as they did. I was wrong. My advice to you is never be so goal driven that you ignore all the external and internal warning signs that maybe that job isn't right for you after all.

Passions

Finally, in this section on Your Higher Self, think about what you are passionate about in life. What moves you, where do you find your greatest joy, what makes your heart race with excitement? Look to your body language for clues – what is it that you do that causes you to exude commitment and delight through the way you move your hands, use your voice or expend your energy? What is it that makes life worth living for you? When you have identified at least six 'passion drivers' write these on your Heartwork Plan in the appropriate place.

"As each tree is individually coded
so each human being has a unique purpose.
We can't buy or inherit our purpose, we have to
develop into it. Achieving this is the only thing
that will give us a feeling of success."
Frances Wilks, Intelligent Emotion

✍ Exercise: Heartwork Plan: Your 'Brand'

Now, let's develop the work you began in Chapter Three, on looking at yourself as a brand. For this we are going to use a marketing exercise usually called a SWOT analysis (for Strengths, Weaknesses, Opportunities and Threats). Only this version is a SUOT analysis because I prefer the word understrengths to weaknesses. Giving yourself a brand identity not only helps you see the bigger picture of what you have to offer the world of work but allows you to stay on top of what your internal (ie, co-workers) and external customers want from you. It is only when you know what people want that you can deliver the goods and maintain their loyalty to you.

While you may be quite clear about your top five strengths and those things you could be better at, when assessing your under-strengths it helps to get some objective feedback from people around you: your partner, close friends or someone at work. It can also be quite an eye-opener because we take for granted many things we do innately, and we may even undervalue aspects of ourselves that others find impressive. On the other hand, you may consider the fact that you are late for everything as an endearing idiosyncracy, whereas others may feel it is holding you back from being taken seriously at work or being more highly valued as an employee or co-worker. Look for the complaints you get consistently from others when completing the 'understrengths' section and be as honest as possible with yourself about what you could improve upon – whether that involves job-related or personal skills – if only you made up your mind to do so.

I suggest leaving the sections headed Opportunities and Threats until you have completed this book. Then you will have a clearer vision of your purpose in life and how that relates to what you want to do in the world of work, beyond material gains like a better salary, prestige and status. Once you have a clear focus on how best you can live your personal values through the work you do, you will undoubtedly find yourself thinking less in terms of what you want, but what service you can offer to others.

Career coach and counsellor Richard Leider, author of

The Power of Purpose, says that one of the three hungers that people try to feed throughout their lives is the knowledge that they matter, that they have left behind some kind of personal mark or legacy. This 'unique thumbprint' is not about ensuring your children get to inherit your bulging bank account or big house when you die, but the creativity behind nurturing, shaping or enhancing others' lives. Once you have found the meaning you choose to give to your life then you will be in a better position to see what action you need to take to develop future opportunities for yourself and recognise those threats that could stop you achieving your goals.

Your Unique Selling Point (USP)

If you hadn't guessed it already, one of the key messages of this book is that you are a unique individual whose life has profound meaning and purpose. In the same way that people like that concierge, photographer, artist and builder mentioned earlier bring their personal signatures to their work, you too have what in marketing parlance is called a Unique Selling Point or USP. This determines the kind of person you choose to be in your work and marks you as different from all the other secretaries, accountants, traffic wardens or shop assistants in the world. Take a look at the personal slogan and logo you wrote during the brand entity exercise (see pages 84–5). In what way does that help you uncover your USP? When you have found it, write it on your Heartwork Plan.

---

*"I think there's a 'sweet spot' that each of us has.
It's the kind of work we want to perform,
the kind of work that makes us proud. But finding
that sweet spot requires deep self-knowledge.
You start by looking at the work you're drawn to.
You try it, you evaluate the experience and you
evolve as you discover more about it."*
**Larry Smith, John F Kennedy School of Government,
Harvard University**

✍ Exercise: Heartwork Plan: Your Future

In our excitement at uncovering the kind of work we wish to do that will engage our souls, it is tempting to forget that the culture in which we operate can have a major impact on whether or not we feel fulfilled. Look once again at your list of the best Life Line experiences and consider what kind of environment contributed to that.

Then think about the people who inspire you, motivate you, make doing whatever you are doing more fulfilling and enjoyable. What are their attitudes and traits? Look beyond the individual to find common threads between all those people you admire, love to be with and work best around. Is a serious workforce the best kind for you, or do you need a place with lots of fun and laughter?

Then consider your ideal environment in a physical sense. Does working in an open-plan office make for an enjoyable and suitable backdrop for your work, or do you prefer the privacy of your own space? Do you feel at ease or stimulated in a concrete jungle or need to be surrounded by clean air and green grass?

When you come to read the following two chapters on money and balance, you might find your preferred environment is closer to home, in the country rather than the city, or in a completely different part of the country or world altogether.

Your *sine qua non* (SQN)

Daphne Rose Kingma introduces the concept of finding your *sine qua non* (a Latin phrase meaning an indispensable condition) in her wonderful book on relationships, *Finding True Love*. This is also relevant to finding the love of your life in the context of your work. When you understand the one requirement you absolutely must have – the one thing you will not compromise on – in order to move forward in any line of work or relationship, you know you have put in place the infrastructure that ensures your deepest needs will be fulfilled.

In the same way that Kingma found that couples needed this 'grounding bond' to be shared in order that each of them accept that other preferences may not be met, it is essential that your SQN be exemplified by whoever or whatever you decide to work for.

But before you can check this out, you need to know what your SQN is: the one aspect of your working life that is not negotiable. For me it is autonomy, the freedom to do things my own way, according to my schedule, but while accepting the need to meet a required objective. For you it could be to do with environmental issues so that you only work for companies that minimise the negative impact of their products; or it could be concerned with family-friendly policies, honesty, spiritual principles or any number of things. Look again at the key words in the core of your values circle (see page 84) and find the one thing you know you cannot live or work without – that non-negotiable 'indispensable condition'. Then, in your scrutiny of organisations that deserve to have you working for them, you can investigate whether that SQN is shared.

✍ Exercise: Studying your Heartwork Plan

Now you have come closer to completing your Heartwork Plan, pin it up somewhere private where you can see it every day, or refer to it before you go to sleep each night. Then allow your subconscious to do the rest. You will undoubtedly find that little hunches come to you in the days and weeks that follow, ideas that you find you can't resist following up.

~ Signposts ~

By fixing these aspects in your mind you will energetically draw to you the people who can help you bring your dream into reality. These are the coincidences or mysterious happenings that life throws our way every so often to prompt us to seek out their higher meaning. Don't shrug your shoulders and say: 'It's just a coincidence'. Think about how that sudden piece of information, that new introduction, that signpost from life, relates to your desire to engage in work that you love. Then follow up those hunches. There is little more action required than that. Let your intuition be your guide and try not to allow your logical left brain to quash any thoughts that come to you just because they don't fit your idea of what is obvious and achievable. Accept that the 'impossible' only remains so when you don't act on your dreams, which might mean taking a slightly indirect route.

Have you ever engaged in those word puzzles where you are presented with two words of the same length but which otherwise are completely different, the object being, by changing just one letter of the word at the top of the list and every subsequent one, to turn it into the new word at the bottom? What slight shifts can you make, within what you do right now, that will move you gradually but inexorably towards work that you love to do for a living? By looking at your Heartwork Plan every day you will begin to formulate and plan the steps you need to take to break down each of your goals into objectives and tasks. In the same way that you wouldn't try to digest a large steak by stuffing it all into your mouth in one go, your goals need to be broken down into manageable 'mouthfuls'.

Finally in this chapter, making a brightly coloured poster of pictures representing your goals is a very powerful way of bringing them a reality. Spend the next week or so looking in magazines for anything that might represent not just the work you desire to do but the lifestyle that you intend to go with it. Cut them out and stick them on to a large coloured piece of card and, again, keep it where you can see it daily. I did this when wishing I could buy a Saab convertible, even though at the time ownership seemed an impossible dream. Within three months I owned one. Not exactly the model I'd really wished for, and certainly not brand new, but one that I am delighted with nevertheless because I detached myself from needing to achieve my goal exactly as I had specified it.

~ Martine's story ~

We often think that individuals who know their vocation and have focused on achieving 'heart work' from an early age have an easier time of it than those who have little or no idea of what they are passionate about. Yet they are faced with tough choices and constant challenges, as this story demonstrates:

Martine had wanted to be an astrologer from the age of 13 when it seemed that her mission in life was being presented to her through a series of serendipitous clues. Her family engaged in a ritual of reading their horoscopes every week in the Sunday newspapers; she found herself most interested in the astrological features in the girls' magazines she bought with her pocket money; and was compelled to seek out books on how to set up a birth chart, even when she'd gone into a bookstore or library for a completely different subject. Martine's earliest recollection of a lifestyle that made perfect sense, and which she subsequently aspired to, was the lead character in a 1970s TV series in which a female astrologer worked with a detective to help solve various crimes. Martine always had the feeling that with astrology she was on familiar territory; it was as if her authentic self had found its perfect means of expression.

After a successful career in television production, during which time she battled daily with the feeling that she should be studying astrology, Martine decided to give in to her soul's demands and left this relatively secure, well-paid and pension-able environment to do exactly that. She met with consider-able opposition from her family of conservative professionals, particularly her mother, who was a solicitor. Against the argument that this was not a 'proper job' for someone of her intelligence and upper middle class background, Martine sim-ply stated that she couldn't battle against herself any longer: she had no choice but to follow her heart, become a coun-selling astrologer and help people understand why life challenged them in certain ways.

Martine has made huge financial sacrifices in following her heart and becoming an astrologer, but says that it never occurs to her to see herself as anything other than an upper-bracket professional – on par with people earning ten times what she does – because of the life-changing, therapeutic value of her work. Martine believes her work is an extension of her-self and that when she says 'I am an astrologer', that tells the other person more about her than just what she does for a liv-ing. She also hopes that in her stylish, articulate, empowering and compassionate way, she is contributing to improving the image of astrologers generally.

AFFIRMATIONS

Now you have had some practise writing affirmations for the
previous three chapters, try penning six to eight of your own
that relate to what it is you really want to do for a living.

✍ Your action list from this chapter

Write down at least six things that you intend to do now – ie, today
not tomorrow – based on what you have learned in this chapter.

1

2

3

4

5

6

"If what you're doing is worth anything, then failing
now and again is inevitable. Ultimately success is
about getting past the setbacks that you encounter."
John Peterman, Chairman and CEO

CHAPTER FIVE

Do you work purely for the money?

"Wealth consciousness, by definition, is a state of mind."
Deepak Chopra, *Creating Affluence*

Money – or rather, what it represents to us in terms of material needs, desires, freedom and choice – is one of the main reasons why people shackle themselves to a job they detest. That, and never having taken the time or effort to discover what it is they really want to do for a living.

Having worked your way through numerous exercises to help with the latter, we now look at what to do about the former. Because until you've got your head around the fear many of us have of being inwardly fulfilled yet outwardly poverty stricken – the stereotypical notion of the impoverished 'artist in the attic' – then you'll not be in the best position to take that leap of faith and embrace your life's mission wholeheartedly, as represented by the work you love.

From the viewpoint of someone who is largely unfulfilled at work, money is hugely important. But that salary is a Bandaid that's been put on a wound that really should receive stitches. The Bandaid holds everything in place for a while but the resulting scar never really heals properly and usually bursts open again at some stage. This frequently (although not exclusively) happens in middle age when you look around at all the wonderful possessions you've accrued and know, in your heart of hearts, that they mean nothing, that they are not enough. Even millionaires – in fact, especially millionaires – aren't exempt from this experience. In his book *Reclaiming Higher Ground*, Lance H K Secretan writes: 'After spending a decade building a business from scratch to $100 million in annual sales, I asked myself the same question others ask in similar situations: "Is this all there is? What's next? $200 million? Isn't there anything more liberating, more meaningful?" '

The answer, as Secretan and others have discovered, is yes: it is work that we do for love, not purely for money. I say 'purely' because I'm the first to admit that money oils the wheels of a more comfortable life. It's what bought me the car of my dreams, which not only enhances my travelling experiences but is tangible proof of what I have achieved by myself. Money is what allows me to pack up my laptop and write, overlooking the Pacific Ocean in Redondo Beach, California, when otherwise I'd be in freezing England. It's what enables me to buy gifts or meals for friends as a supplement to saying 'Thank you' or 'I love you'.

But when money becomes the be-all and end-all of life then you are guilty of gagging your soul rather than be disturbed by its whispering entreaties to stop allowing your Ego (remember, the acronym for Everything Good's Outside) to control your life. It's not your ego that will hold your hand on the path to enlightenment, but your soul. Your ego needs to be constantly engaged in the acquisition of money in order to bolster up its fragility. Which reminds me of a distant relative whom I was told collects rare old coins. Only, instead of giving himself the pleasure of enjoying them, he keeps them in a vault in his bank. He rationalises this by saying they are too valuable to even be in his house, and having spent so much money on them over the years, he is constantly afraid of having them stolen. So there they stay, in the vault, gathering dust. To which any sane person might ask, 'Why? What's the point of having beautiful things if you can't enjoy them?' Merely possessing something won't confer wealth, it's the value you create in using it.

The same is true of your life, the most beautiful and value-creating 'thing' you will ever possess. Maintaining the treadmill of doing work you loathe – or at best are indifferent to – in order to feel secure, prevents you from fully enjoying this amazing experience. Let passion, not pounds, propel you in life and not only will your new mindset diminish the current appeal of financial wealth, but ironically you will become so compelling that you will attract all the money you need anyway. The alternative is the desolation of finding that you've spent half or more of your life climbing the ladder of material success only to discover it's been up against the wrong wall all along.

~ Overcoming fear ~

Before we begin some exercises around money and what it represents to you, let's take a moment to examine what underpins the desire to earn money to the exclusion of almost everything else: fear.

There are a number of different types of fear, but here are three that are most closely associated with money.

Fear of failure

This fear centres around not letting ourselves and those we care for down, not wishing to look like losers in front of others, not wishing to embrace the embarrassment of not meeting society's definition of success. Not earning enough money, particularly if we are with a partner who is very money oriented, comes under this category. However, we are rarely talking about survival; simply status and prestige, which are socially determined. There was probably a time, as there has been for most of us, when you got by on considerably less than you do now. Possibly your relationship with your partner was more fulfilling as a result. If you could only free yourself from the notion that earning less equates to failure then you might realise you can manage very well on a lower salary and take a lot of pressure off yourself into the bargain.

When I left work to have my first child we lost half our income almost overnight. I used to joke that I should write a book entitled *101 Ways with Minced Beef* because it was about the only meat we could then afford. I turned every shopping expedition into a challenge to see how well we could eat on less. Ironically, now that I can afford to buy smoked salmon and the best cuts of meat, shopping seems much more of a meaningless chore.

Fear of success

This is as common as the fear of failure. What if you do become happier and wealthier? Won't your friends be jealous, won't everyone hate you for 'having it all'? Won't you drive yourself insane by eternally asking why you deserve all this when those around you have to manage on much less?

Financial success in particular can be a terrifying prospect for many people because they believe it will set them apart from the life they have always known. And without the proper foresight and planning it often does, which is why so many lottery winners are so miserable. It also means that you have to take responsibility for your life and face some major self-esteem issues around deserving and 'not being good enough'.

I urge you to read again Marianne Williamson's fine words on pages 31–2. Maybe you have been programmed to believe that everyone who is successful and rich got to be that way because they are complete bastards and uncaring, ruthless monsters. But then, maybe it is part of your life's mission to demonstrate the complete opposite.

Fear of the unknown

Now we get to the real biggie. Fear, of course, is a close relation of risk, which is why some people never take that step of changing their lives for the better. Better the devil you know, as the saying goes. Fear, in many respects, is necessary to our survival. Fear of being attacked causes us not to walk alone in certain parts of the city late at night, for example. Fear of getting burned ensures we keep our hands away from blazing objects. But we are dogged by so many unfounded fears, too. These are like the shadows on a wall that suggest a big, scary monster is coming to get you when in fact it's just your neighbour's cat who wants to be friendly. You are reacting to what you think is there, not what actually is there. Being afraid of the future – which is what fear of the unknown boils down to – is senseless when you accept that you create your future with the thoughts you are having right now and with every act that you commit or fail to commit.

Try thinking the way an Olympic athlete does. They set themselves a realistic time limit, for example competing at the next games in four years' time. They focus on a compelling goal: whether that's to run a certain distance in a record-breaking time or to exceed their personal best. Then they break that goal down into small, incremental objectives and tasks so that every week, every month, every year they are gradually moving closer towards achieving their medal. Each objective helps them determine what internal and external resources they need to draw on to ensure their success. Failure is disappointing, sure, but it is simply a measure of whether or not all the right resources are in place at a given time.

No athlete would expect to knock several seconds off his or her best time in one fell swoop. Similarly, you shouldn't put undue pressure on yourself by trying to achieve too much too soon. Trust that, if you have read the signs right, you are on the right path to achieving your heart's desire in your work and then detach yourself from a specific outcome, particularly in an unrealistic time frame.

As we have discussed before, you can choose the meaning of the events in your life. Risk can become challenge, fear can become a catalyst for growth, an indication that you are facing another major life challenge that will lead you closer to personal fulfilment. And failure can become feedback, an opportunity to reappraise your tactics so you don't make the same 'mistake' next time.

A risk a day keeps the fear away

Make a list of things you can start doing today that will get you into the habit of breaking out of your comfort zone and stretch you into taking more risks. Here's a few to start:

- Change a ritual, such as the time you get up in the morning, the route you take to work, the fact that you always have your parents over to Sunday lunch
- Say no, without offering an explanation, to anything you really don't want to do
- When someone asks you for the truth, be truthful
- Be the person who starts a fun programme at your place of work (see Chapter Six)
- Express how you feel when someone hurts, disappoints or angers you
- Tell someone you love them
- Speak out publicly on a subject you feel passionate about
- Ask someone out
- Say you're sorry
- Tell someone you disagree with them.

✑ Exercise: Breaking patterns in your mind

Your imagination is one place where you can take risks safely.
Find somewhere quiet where you won't be disturbed for a few
hours. Take the phone off the hook. Put a 'Do not disturb' sign on
the door and arm yourself with whatever you need to create a
warm, safe and inspiring environment. Allow yourself to sit
quietly for a few minutes, letting your thoughts float through your
mind like clouds. Acknowledge them but don't focus on any one
particular thought or issue. Be aware of your breath and try to
inhale slowly and deeply through your nose, exhaling nasally also.

Now think of a situation that involves an element of risk for
you. You may want to try this exercise with a small risk to start
with, or consider the risk of leaving your current employment to
follow your vocational path. Whatever you choose to think about,
imagine it as fully as you can: take your mind into the future and
'see' yourself in the situation that you currently fear. What
smells, tastes or other sensations are associated with these new
circumstances? Using all your senses to make them seem as
real as possible, reflect on these questions:

● What is the worst thing that could happen if you took this risk?
● How would you be able to deal with that?
● What emotions are coming up and what are they based on?
  Old wounds, childhood fears, social 'rules' that you fear
  breaking? Can you accept that these are past attitudes and
  behaviours and have no relevance to your future life – the
  one you want to live from now on?
● In what ways could you limit your worst case scenario and
  maximise your chances of a positive outcome?
● What is the positive outcome of such a risk and how does this
  stack up against the negative for you? Which is the more
  compelling scenario?

Think of your mind as a mental sports field or stage. You can set
the rules for the game as well as the script for the play.
Experiment with many different possibilities as you did with
Scenario Planning (see page 90). All the time, be aware of the
sensations that occur in your body: these are the clues to how
congruent your imagined actions are with your true Self.

When you've answered the above questions to your satisfaction, then it's time to plan how to bring that previously perceived 'risky situation' into reality by setting out the steps you
need to take to ensure a successful outcome. Remember Max
Gunther's traits of lucky people (page 62)? One of these is taking calculated risks. No one would ask you to jump out of an
aeroplane without first securing your parachute, or checking
that you have one fitted. Letting go of the fear of being without money involves taking well-planned risks, with you having thought through how you will manage on a day-to-day
basis until your venture gets off the ground.

You are in control; no matter how compelling the desire to
do something different with your life, you can decide the best
time to let go of your old ways of working and embrace a new
one. Remember that we have free will. That is what the Bible
story of Adam and Eve is all about: giving up the instinctual
world of animals for the more complicated and painful but
hugely liberating arena of moral choice.

A further factor in achieving economic security, while at the
same time minimising the hold that money has over you, is to
consider another of the 'luck factors': cutting your losses
quickly. When you have discovered and decide to embark on
your true vocation, life has a habit of giving you the green
light by serendipitously bringing you into contact with just the
right people, in just the right places, at just the right time.
However, this isn't the case forever. Remember what I wrote
about being a spiritual warrior (see page 7) who undergoes
difficulties and sacrifices in order to test whether you are
courageous enough to claim the glittering prizes in life?
Spiritual warriors need to attune themselves to the signs life
throws in their path from time to time. This means being
aware of red lights as well as green ones; stopping yourself
going down a path that isn't working out for you; and getting
out of situations that don't feel right. Retreat isn't always a
backwards step – it can move you forward too.

The higher your self-esteem and the deeper your motivation, the more you will want to ensure you reach your destination, to achieve your goals, to succeed in your life's mission.
Never jeopardise that by foolishly embarking on a new life
until you:

- Are sure you have all the emotional resources to cope
- Have worked out the minimum you will need to live on, and have some finances in reserve to see you through the early days (the exercises on page 129–32 are designed to help you with this)
- Have demonstrated the resourcefulness of scenario planning and have alternative routes up your sleeve in case the first one you try results in a dead-end
- Fully appreciate that living according to your personal values and inner motivations can sometimes involve many financial and emotional sacrifices.

~ The meaning of money ~

Money is a means to an end. It has no value other than that which we place on it. And the most meaningful value money has is for pleasurable experiences, such as the memories of that holiday of a lifetime, that beautiful house you enjoy living in, the dream car that makes driving a pleasure, the chance to give your children an excellent education. These are much more valuable ways of spending money than keeping old masters, rare coins or priceless jewellery locked away for fear that someone might damage or steal them.

When it boils down to it, money is all about emotions. It is commonly about control, power, choice, freedom, or love. Find the emotion that underpins the meaning of money for you and you will either discover that money is a poor example of that need or that you are able to think of an alternative means of supply.

Let's take the issue of control, for example. Control and security are closely linked. Yet money as a form of security is an illusion. Often the financially wealthiest individuals are the most insecure, as the example of my coin-collecting relative demonstrated. How can money equate to security when it can so easily be taken from you? It can be stolen, lost, the stock-market could crash, as it did so famously in 1929, it can be devalued by the government, and so on. True security – in fact the only security there is – comes from the knowledge that you can handle any situation you are faced with, any time you have to. Such self-confidence is priceless.

You cannot control other people with money. It may buy you company, begrudging gratitude, or sex, but it can never buy real love. Parents often substitute money for love and time then are appalled when their children do the same to them decades later, perhaps by paying for home care but never visiting them, except perhaps at Christmas.

Think about what money means to you emotionally and how valid its connection with that emotion really is. Then look inside yourself and ask what further inner work you need to undertake to replace your need for the external riches of money when true happiness can only be achieved by investing in the inner resources of the soul.

~ Spiritual abundance and ~ earthly pragmatism

In our quantum reality, money is a form of energy: just like your body, the chair you are sitting on, or your thoughts. As Deepak Chopra outlines in *Creating Affluence*, so-called material things are simply different arrangements of energy and information. Energy is meant to flow; indeed, the word currency comes from the Latin *currens* meaning to circulate. There is an ebb and flow about money as there is in all things in life. In stockmarket terms there are bull markets and bear markets; in governmental terms there are boom times and periods of recession; money flows into our bank accounts when we get paid and out again when there are large bills to see to (which, if your experience is anything like mine, always tend to come at the same time). Like the concept of yin and yang, light and dark, good and evil, the spiritual laws that govern money are dependent on the cyclical nature of our reality. The trick is to encourage this natural flow by giving, while at the same time keeping enough money back to cover you through the lean times.

There are two popular New Age approaches to money that are not mutually exclusive and work well if you combine them. The first is that of prosperity consciousness, as advocated by the likes of Napoleon Hill and Deepak Chopra, and is the subject of books such as *The Seven Laws of Money*, *The Dynamic Laws of Prosperity* and *Creating Money: Keys to Abundance*. The second is voluntary simplicity, advocated by writers such as Sarah Ban Breathnach and Elaine St James. The first, more metaphysical, approach involves thinking abundantly in order to reflect the natural state of a generous universe and attract prosperity in all its forms. The second offers a pragmatic approach to living on less, or at least within your means, which makes good sense since frugality is a practice well known to most millionaires.

The ancient practice of tithing is an early example of prosperity consciousness. It recognised the symbolic life energy of money and ensured it flowed outwards as well as inwards, because in spiritual terms abundance comes from meeting others' needs. Tithing means giving away 10 per cent of your income, either to a charity or a religious organisation or someone with needs greater than your own. Combine that with thriftier living and you would then cream off and save a further 10 per cent of your income, again on a regular basis. By doing this you are taking practical steps to ensure that, when you do decide to make major life changes, the financial implications don't hinder you as much as they might because you have created a safety net for yourself. Most of us could live on far less than we do and, as you will discover from the financial planning exercises later in this chapter, making changes now can help reduce the fear of enforced changes in your lifestyle.

The two-income family is increasingly the norm these days yet families continue to find themselves in poor financial shape. Could this not be because 'saving for a rainy day' has largely gone out of fashion? In North America, the wealthiest nation on earth, saving represents just 4.8 per cent of the average income and more than one million Americans file for bankruptcy every year. The 'want it now, pay for it later' culture is endemic. In Britain it is estimated that millions of people will still be paying off credit-card debts in July for presents they bought the previous Christmas. Yet frugality, as advocated by US newsletter *The Tightwad Gazette* helped one couple, with an annual income of under $30,000, to save $49,000 in seven years, in addition to spending $38,000 on cars and furniture – and stay out of debt. They were even able to buy a $125,000 farmhouse with seven acres of land in Maine. Their secret was in making the distinction between 'investment purchases' that hold their value and 'disposable purchases' that largely represent meaningless consumption. In the same way that Robert (see page 41) turned even the most mind-numbing and menial tasks into games and challenges, you can choose to view a more economical way of living as fun. As Arnold Bennett said: 'Much ingenuity with a little money is vastly more profitable and amusing than much money without ingenuity.'

Think of your money as you would any other possession and apply some Feng Shui principles to it. This ancient Chinese concept advocates regular spates of clutter clearing in order to ensure that the flow of energy in your home or office doesn't become stagnated, leading to bad luck or ill health. Similarly, get into the habit of 'clearing' the energy in your bank accounts by moving it about, particularly by giving some away to those who are needier than yourself. Are you really poor or just subjecting yourself to poverty consciousness? Gratitude for what you have and generosity towards others are two of the spiritual keys of happiness. Be grateful and give – and get back into rhythm with the natural ebb and flow of the laws of prosperity.

~ Why be rich when you can be wealthy? ~

Myths and legends are full of stories of characters who lusted after money at the expense of their souls. King Midas' desire for greater riches became a curse when even the simple pleasures such as kissing his daughter or eating and drinking turned into a living nightmare because everything he touched turned into gold. Midas was then forgiven by the gods, who told him to wash everything in water to turn it back to its pre-gold state, because he recognised that what we take for granted – including continuing good health, love, friendship – is far more valuable than money. Similarly, Scrooge, in Dickens' *A Christmas Carol*, was dead to the joys of living when we meet him early in the book but changes his tactics when he sees the horrors awaiting him in the future.

What these and other stories reinforce is the fact that abundance or prosperity isn't synonymous with financial riches. People who are happy with their lives; follow their heart in their work; enjoy good health; have a loving partner, family and supportive friends; and take a positive, carefree attitude will always be considered 'wealthier' than a lonely, miserable, cancer-ridden billionaire whose life is only populated by hangers-on. Money can buy you no end of marvellous possessions, but if after acquiring them you still don't feel happy, then perhaps it's time to accumulate the riches of the soul. The following case study illustrates how one man found it possible to work from the heart without money holding him back.

"If money were the key to happiness, millionaires wouldn't have ulcers. They do and it's not."
Dr Joy Brown,
The Nine Fantasies That Will Ruin Your Life

~ Michael's story ~

With his Irishman's 'gift of the gab' and love of people, Michael had been a successful independent financial consultant for more years than he cared to remember. He also had enjoyed his work, until his company was swallowed up by a larger organisation with a voracious appetite for greater profits. Soon ever-increasing targets began to wear him down. Rather than risk being out of step with his personal values of honesty and integrity Michael decided to quit – not just his job, but the industry. At 45 years of age something was nagging him that it was time to find greater fulfilment doing something else. Working long, stressful hours had put a strain on his marriage, he rarely had the time or energy for his children and hadn't picked up a squash racket in years.

When Michael saw an advertisement in his local newspaper for postal workers, he felt inexplicably drawn to apply. His

wife's reaction echoed the nagging voice he was desperately
trying to shut off in his own head: that this was a comedown
in his career, they'd never live off the money, what would their
friends think? But Michael knew, in his heart of hearts, that
he wanted to find work where, at the end of the day, he could
leave his cares behind. He wanted a job with less stress and
more exercise, that would bring him into contact with many
different people, offering a service beyond simply delivering
letters, and give him the chance to repair his relationship with
his wife and teenage sons.

From the moment he donned his postman's uniform
Michael felt as if he had come home. His colleagues were
friendlier and more sociable than those he'd been used to in
the insurance company he'd worked for. He became a popular caller with many older residents who would ask the 'young
man' to help them with minor odd jobs – which he was
delighted to do. Michael and his wife began to write down
every single purchase and expense made over a three-month
period, and were appalled at how profligate they were used to
being. Every packet of crisps, every evening paper or packet
of chewing gum was recorded and then totalled weekly under
various headings to see where savings might be made.

By starting work early in the mornings, Michael was at
home when his sons returned from college. They got into the
habit of going down to the local leisure centre as a family,
enjoying the facilities at cheaper off-peak rates. Michael and
his wife even rediscovered the joys of afternoon sex.

The combination of a strengthened sense of family, supportive co-workers, no stress, physical exercise and a feeling
of being part of the community meant that Michael has never
looked back or wished he'd hung on to his old life. In fact, he
often wonders how he ever stuck it out for so long. The satisfaction he feels about his life now more than makes up for
his drop in salary. Ironically, by being more 'economically
conscious' as he puts it, Michael and his family have been able
to save for a dream holiday in Australia to visit a brother he
hasn't seen in over 20 years.

✍ Exercise: Financial planning

Copy the chart on pages 130–1.

In the left-hand column is a list of everyday household expenses. Add any that relate to your lifestyle and are missing.

The next three columns are where you should enter the relevant figures. The first is 'Current Expenses' and you should outline what you currently spend in each of these areas. If you don't know what that is, try doing what Michael's family did and make a note of all your expenses – major and minor – for a month.

The second column is headed 'Making Savings'. Enter in these columns what you estimate you might spend if you thought a little more about your monthly expenditure.

The third column reads 'Voluntary Simplicity'. What is the minimum amount you could live on? What if you could live without all those magazine subscriptions, the West End hair-dressing bills, the duplicated insurance policies? How much could you save if you bought at thrift shops in good areas, took the bus instead of taxis, bought in bulk with your neighbours, let the membership to that private health club you never go to lapse and visit public amenities instead? What could you manage on if you really had to?

Turn this exercise into a game and challenge yourself to find greater savings until you have pared this down to the bare minimum.

"Happiness is not having what you want,
but wanting what you have."
Anon

Financial Planning Chart

Outgoings	Current Expenses
Rent/Mortgage	
Gas/Electricity	
Oil/Coal	
Water Rates	
Council Tax	
Insurances:	
Buildings	
Contents	
Life cover	
Pension plan	
Health	
Car maintenance	
Car loan	
Season ticket(s)	
Petrol	
Road tax	
Savings plan	
Investments/other	
TV licence	
Clothing	
Home repairs/maintenance	
Christmas & birthdays gifts	
Subscriptions	
Memberships	
Food/drink (incl. meals out)	
Home telephone(s)	
Mobile telephone(s)	
Social life/outings	
Childcare	
Education/tuition	
Car parking	
Dry cleaning	
Newspapers & magazines	
Hair care	
Postage	
Accountant's fees	
Other professional fees	
Cable/satellite TV rental	
Medical/dental fees	
Holidays	
Pet care	
OTHERS	

Making Savings	Voluntary Simplicity

✎ Exercise: The cost of work

Use the chart on pages 130–1 to estimate your total outgoings every month. Analyse how much of that is related to your work and the expenses it incurs. These areas could include the cost of:

- rail travel or petrol
- clothing (suits, tights, shoes, etc)
- entertaining and lunches
- your time travelling to and from work
- healthcare for any work-related illnesses you have suffered
- additional taxes paid on company benefits such as your car
- housing: could you move to a less expensive area if you didn't need ready access to your work?

Now look at how much less you would need to earn to pay for what is left.

One of the greatest riches in life is having fun. How much fun do you have in your working life right now? If there is very little, the next chapter will give you plenty of ideas for changing that sorry situation.

"Tell your heart that the fear of suffering is worse than the suffering itself. And that no heart has ever suffered when it goes in search of its dreams, because every second of the search is a second's encounter with God and with eternity."
Paulo Coelho, **The Alchemist**

AFFIRMATIONS

✔ Every day in every way I am becoming more and more prosperous.
✔ Money is starting to hold less attraction for me when compared with my health, the love of my partner/family, with friendship.
✔ I am becoming more adept at finding and enjoying the simple pleasures in life.
✔ My attitude is changing to one of wealth consciousness in all its forms.
✔ I am choosing to live a happier, more fulfilling life rather than one that is fixated on earning money.
✔ Honouring the spiritual laws of prosperity means giving a proportion of what I earn to those who need it.
✔ I am recognising the need to become more grateful for all the benefits in my life, including financial ones.

✍ Your action list from this chapter

Write down at least six things that you intend to do now – ie, today not tomorrow – based on what you have learned in this chapter.

1
2
3
4
5
6

Why isn't your working life more fun?

"What then is the right way to live? Life should be lived as play."
Plato

Fun: joy, pleasure, entertainment, merriment, cheer. For the vast majority the phrase 'a fun company' is an oxymoron. Because fun is so often confused with frivolity, defined as silly, unintelligent, senseless behaviour, it is considered not to be appropriate in the workplace. Yet the word silly comes from the Greek *selig* meaning blessed.

Educational psychologists know that play is an important way for children to learn about the world, to expand their creativity and feel good about themselves. Today's so-called learning organisations – the ones who say they want employees who are knowledgeable, creative and confident – could learn a lot, and benefit hugely, from encouraging more fun in the workplace.

The Protestant work ethic causes us to compartmentalise fun as something we should only do outside of work. The very word work, with its connotations of toil, drudgery and effort, conspires to eliminate fun, laughter and play from what we do for a living. But, again, this is only because we continue to accept that kind of attitude and behaviour as normal. If you consider giving your car its weekly wash to be a leisure activity, you will discover the pleasure in transforming the grimy paintwork back to a showroom gleam, as well as appreciating the rare opportunity to let your mind wander freely while doing so. However, if you approach the same task as work, it's unlikely you'll get any joy out of it.

Having fun at work doesn't have to involve zaniness, practical jokes and everyone acting like a Butlin's Redcoat, but simply deciding to take it upon ourselves to encourage more smiling, more laughter, greater honesty and respect in our interactions with others – in short, more humanity. A happy workplace is the responsibility of each one of us; we just have to decide to stick our necks out and be the first person to commit to making a difference. This would not only reduce the astounding number of stressed-out individuals who contribute to the ever-increasing amount of sickness absence in business today, but would lead to a much more creative and productive working environment.

Psychologists have found that humour in the workplace has many functions, namely:

- is a beneficial outlet for frustration and stress
- breaks down barriers between people, laughter being a universal 'language'
- strengthens relationships
- reduces boredom
- consolidates group identity
- reduces the effects of controlled environments
- increases enjoyment of even menial tasks
- reduces tension
- enhances self-image and social identity
- reinforces a sense of belonging.

It is for these reasons that humour is commonly practised in hierarchical organisations where there are often long periods of either repetitive work or inactivity, such as in factories, the police force or the fire brigade. Without it, the workforce might just go insane.

As Norman Cousins outlined in his book *The Anatomy of an Illness*, a genuine belly laugh eases pain, cures insomnia, restores a sense of faith and hope (and sanity) to one's life and is, after all, a free activity we each can engage in anywhere. Laughter releases a wealth of natural painkilling hormones into the body to relax muscles and give the nervous system, inner organs and respiratory system a virtual 'internal massage'. It is also believed to increase levels of Immunoglobulin A, an essential antibody that helps your system fight against infection and disease.

~ Fun and creativity ~

Anyone looking to enhance their creativity at work can do no
better than inject some fun, laughter and play into their working environment. These are all vital factors, particularly for
you if one of your important 'personal needs' from the exercise in the Introduction is 'socialising with co-workers'.

As someone once said: 'Creativity involves looking at the
same thing as everyone else and thinking something different.'
This explains why young children, who are immensely creative, rarely use toys in the way manufacturers intended them
to be used, or play with the box instead, because that doesn't
limit their self-expression. Reverting to child-like (not to be
confused with child-ish) behaviour allows you to get rid of the
labels and rules that stifle our innate creativity - an attribute
embracing flexibility, originality and open-mindedness that
will enhance your employability.

The following are just three examples of companies that
recognise that fun is an asset to any organisation.

~ Case study: Allied Domecq ~

As a company in the business of selling enjoyment, the international spirits and retail group Allied Domecq has teamed up
with the Royal Shakespeare Company (which it sponsors) to
add a powerful new dimension to its training sessions by
applying theatrical techniques to business needs. Allied
Domecq has found that within a relaxed, fun workshop environment, its employees demonstrate greater courage in facing
the challenges they meet daily in their working lives, which
then has a positive impact on the business as a whole. Team-
building exercises, borrowed from initiatives used by theatre
directors to pull together an ensemble of actors prior to
rehearsals and the production itself, include playing a silent
version of musical chairs; balancing canes between two people's heads; and creating a 'living tableau' in which everyone's
position, facial expression and gestures capture their current
position within a specific business situation.

Delegates may be asked to narrate a business 'story' in the
manner of a fairy tale for pre-school children, make presen-

tations in the style of a theatrical production, or recite nursery rhymes while focusing – not on the words – but on trying to elicit a particular emotion from the listener. Within Allied Domecq, playing games during otherwise formal training workshops not only breaks down barriers between the different departments or teams involved and actively demonstrates the company values of openness, honesty and informality, but, the company believes, is critical to the learning process.

~ Case study: Yo!Sushi ~

The fun starts at Yo!Sushi even before you join the company. The application form for Simon Woodroffe's restaurant business asks questions such as: 'What animal would you choose to be?', 'What bugs you?' and 'What's the greatest thing about you?' The company doesn't hire on the basis of these answers but finds that the form is a light-hearted way of breaking down barriers in an otherwise formal process.

Yo!Sushi management sets great store on encouraging personal expression from its staff, albeit within a structured framework. It's okay for employees to stand on tables and shout 'Yo!' across the restaurant to enhance the relaxed party mood. On one occasion a waitress, overhearing that it was a customer's birthday, turned the music off, got up on a table and orchestrated a spontaneous rendition of 'Happy Birthday' from the other 150 people dining there. She knew she didn't need to ask anyone's permission to do so. The kitchen staff have competitions to see how high a pile of plates they can limbo with under the entrance to the show kitchen. If a few get broken in the process, so what? They can always be replaced, whereas staff camaraderie is a much rarer commodity.

The company hosts regular parties for its staff and one summer took a group of them on a highly organised mystery adventure that ended up in a Surrey forest. This involved being led blindfold in a chain, holding hands and sitting talking or playing games around a bonfire until the early hours.

Managing director Simon Woodroffe believes strongly that organised games is an essential part of the team-building process and breaks down barriers between people.

~ Case study: Air Miles ~

Within Air Miles is a department called Fun Inc, run by volunteers who take time off from their day-to-day responsibilities to come up with creative ways to bring people together 'off the job'. The company organises special occasion parties where the CEO dresses up, and four times a year it brings together the entire workforce from 5pm to midnight for a barbecue and disco; that is in addition to the Christmas party.

The company boasts of being obsessed with thank yous, so much so that three years ago it introduced the concept of Thank You vouchers. Every member of staff receives a book of vouchers, each of which is worth ten Air Miles. When a colleague has done something worthy of note – for example, co-operating over and above the call of duty, making the working day happier and more fulfilling, or supporting the team in some special way – aside from a verbal 'thank you' he or she can be given one of these vouchers. The recipient then sends it into a central administration point and can build up Air Miles credits towards any number of treats, including free flights to anywhere in the world.

A further initiative that Air Miles intends to bring in shortly recognises that the one thing most people feel is at a premium is time. They have come up with the idea of Time Off vouchers, to be awarded hierarchically by someone's assessor in recognition of that little bit extra injected into work. Depending on their value, these vouchers can be used to take off any time from work, from a Friday afternoon to several days in a row.

"Having fun at work depends on loving our work. This means doing something we love. There is no point in slaving in a hell-hole until the age of 65, only to be able to say, 'Phew, glad that's over!'"
Lance H K Secretan

~ Thirty-one 'happiness/fun' ideas ~

Here are some ideas for your workplace: one for every day of the month.

- Transform your meetings into playful occasions. Copy an idea developed at supermarket group Asda and hold meetings without chairs. Alternatively, ask delegates to wear blindfolds; or encourage everyone to wear different coloured hats that designate a particular role for the speakers, so that whoever gets the yellow hat has to play Devil's Advocate, while wearing the red hat means you have to present your ideas with passion.

- Start the day with a rousing sing-song. Who could feel miserable and bad-tempered after a departmental rendition of the Butch Cassidy and the Sundance Kid film theme tune 'Raindrops Keeping Falling on my Head?'

- Take a humour break once a week in which co-workers are invited to share their favourite office jokes or funny stories. Start an 'Office joke of the Week' competition.

- Launch 'Give Someone a Hug Day', and as well as saying thank you for a job well done, give your colleagues a hug. The power of human touch can never be underestimated.

- Lobby your company to offer Joy Grants – vouchers backed up with enough money from petty cash to cover the cost of a nice bottle of wine, a lunchtime snack, a box of chocolates, cinema ticket, or whatever – and award them to anyone who has spread a little happiness in your workplace.

- Start your team get-togethers with an appreciation circle in which each person gets to hear what everyone else values about them.

- Encourage your CEO or departmental heads to fulfil a dare each time your team exceeds a challenging target.

- Try a different approach with presentations on technical or complicated subjects. Suggest they are made in the manner of a children's story in which the audience is a group of five year olds. If they don't understand the language used the presenter has to go back to the drawing board and present his/her message in a simpler way.

- Start a joy list and ask everyone to contribute a sentence or two on why they like working for the company. If the list is depressingly short, do something about it.
- Run a competition for the funniest or cleverest anagram of the company name or that of the CEO.
- Borrow an idea beloved of schools and have a themed casual dress day every so often in which everyone is invited to wear their most embarrassing gear from the 70s or 80s (or even the 60s).
- Start up a social club and ask for ideas for fun nights out: go line dancing or organise a 'pub quiz' evening.
- Turn one of your meeting rooms into a play room with wooden bricks, play dough, paint and paper: anything that will stimulate creativity and relaxation and be a welcome respite from a stressful day.
- Get everyone to bring in a picture of themselves as a baby or small child and pin them on their jackets for a day, or guess which child is which co-worker.
- Ask everyone in your team or department to write a paragraph outlining something surprising about themselves. Offer a prize to whoever comes up with the most outrageous example. It could be an eccentric weekend activity they regularly indulge in, an unusual qualification, a secret desire to live on a Hebridean island, a very different kind of job they once held, the fact that they have six foster children, etc. Type these up and paste them on a board, each one labelled with a letter of the alphabet. Alongside, include a numbered list of all those taking part in the exercise and ask colleagues to try to match the individuals they know with the descriptions given. You could ask them to contribute a small amount of money for every entry they put forward. This not only achieves a stronger link between our working and our authentic selves and helps colleagues get to know each other better, but will undoubtedly be a talking point in the building for months to come.
- Lobby your Human Resources department to re-vamp its rewards and incentives strategy so that these better reflect the individual interests of the staff: such as motor racing

for a day, sky-diving, a pampering day at a top health spa, etc. Also, remind them that people are not always motivated by material rewards. Sometimes they simply want to feel they are valued by getting company-wide recognition such as a write-up about themselves in the departmental newsletter or company magazine, or having their own page on the intranet site for a week.

- Encourage the CEO, board or departmental heads to dress up as 16th-century serving wenches and wait at tables during the Christmas party.
- Start team get-togethers with a challenging, fun, 'bonding' exercise. Try blowing up several packets of balloons and, with just the use of sticky tape, see which group can erect the highest free-standing balloon structure in under five minutes.
- Ensure everyone gets to know new employees by asking them to present a version of an introductions exercise I often use before workshops. 'Coat of Arms' requires them to draw a shield with four sections plus a scroll underneath.

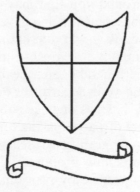

In the four sections they illustrate
1   A recent creative output
2   How they like to spend their spare time
3   Something they are very good at
4   Something about themselves that not many people know.
In the scroll underneath ask them to write a slogan for themselves, their personal philosophy or what they would like to have as their epitaph.

- Determine to be joyful today without needing to have anything special happen.
- Start a buddy system for new employees. Team them up with someone and ensure there's enough money in the kitty to pay for them to have a drink together once after work.
- Have a set of boxing gloves and a punch bag somewhere in the building so that in times of severe stress there's always a physical opportunity to get rid of harmful tension before it builds up in the body.
- Lobby for a masseuse or reflexologist to visit your premises once a month and draw lots or sell raffle tickets to see who is the lucky recipient that week.
- Arrange to give an annual 'Academy Awards' dinner and find a way in which everyone is recognised for something positive.
- Ask staff to offer free lunchtime presentations in which they share their specific, outside-of-work skills, such as origami, feats of memory, a dance routine they can teach everyone, a magic trick, etc. You will be amazed at the untapped talent around you that may even come in handy in a working context some day.
- Ask everyone to think up an alternative mission statement for your company that pokes fun at the pomposity of these often indecipherable and meaningless offerings.
- Offer a prize within your department or team for the owner of the most hideous or talked-about tie in a month.
- Put up large sheets of paper on the toilet walls and encourage removable graffiti: written or drawn.
- Elicit responses to certain proposed initiatives that require a simple yes or no by providing a large number of coloured balls and two baskets. Employees can then register their feelings by placing a red ball in one basket for no or a green ball in the second basket for yes.
- Do what TV production teams do at the end of the year when they scour the cuttings room for the 'bloopers' that got away. Ask each department or team to write and present the funniest, most ridiculous or ironic thing that has happened in the company over the past twelve months and put it on as lunchtime entertainment.

• Get someone in to teach people how to breathe properly and alert them to the fact that when a certain noise sounds in the office, this is the prompt for them to check their breathing.

"Laughter is the shortest distance between two people."
Victor Borge

~ Become a 'happychondriac' ~

Decide today to become what laughter expert Robert Holden calls a 'happychondriac': someone who looks for reasons to be happy rather than miserable. Since our realities are self-created you have nothing to lose but your frown lines.

Ten steps to happiness in the workplace

1 **Accentuate the positive**. Look for what is good in people and situations. If you can't find anything positive to say about your co-workers or job, do something about it – or leave.

2 **Smile, laugh, joke**. Be the person who radiates sunshine; it's infectious and you won't be on your own for long. Even scientifically oriented psychologists recognise what they term 'emotional contagion'.

3 **Put relationships first**. Take the time to understand the person you are dealing with at any moment and try to find a common vision, goal, or purpose. If you commit yourself to always putting relationships before the task, you will find how much easier and pleasant your working life becomes.

4 **Pay compliments**. Saying 'Well done', 'Thank you', 'You look particularly nice today', or 'That tie/shoes/suit really looks good on you' costs nothing but is invaluable to the recipient.

 .5 **Do unto others ...** Look back at page 56 and remember
   that if you want people to be warm, friendly, co-operative,
   helpful, supportive, then you need to act that way yourself. As Ralph Waldo Emerson advised: 'Be the change
   you want to see in the world.'

 6 **Enjoy each moment**. What's going on for you right now is
   called the present because it's a gift. You will have no
   other moment exactly like it ever again. Focus on what
   you can do to make the here and now a valued memory
   and not just a blur in your race towards an uncertain
   future.

 7 **Respond with enthusiasm**. When someone asks you how
   you are, stop responding with 'Not bad, thanks', or
   'Could be better'. Words are powerful tools for self-
   transformation. Unless it is important for someone to
   know that things are not good with you, try saying that
   you feel fantastic. Too often we get caught up in habitual
   negativity that pulls us and the person we are speaking to
   down when it isn't an accurate reflection of how we feel
   at that moment.

 8 **Show your gratitude**. Don't be one of the vast majority
   who only have something to say when it involves finding
   fault. A flower from your garden, a small bar of someone's favourite chocolate or a handwritten note saying,
   'Thanks, you really helped me out' can transform someone's day – and your own.

 9 **Merge work and play**. Turn work into your personal devotion to life, your contribution to fun, creativity and happiness – for yourself and everyone around you.

10 **Commit to bringing your heart to work**. There's an
   inspiring story in *Chicken Soup for the Soul at Work*
   (see Further Reading) in which a trainer found the
   tele-marketing staff of a large US firm to be lacking in
   commitment for learning some new sales technology,
   because they were so dispirited from being treated poorly
   by their boss. His interpersonal skills left a lot to be
   desired, always considering the bottom line to be of
   paramount importance. Discussing the problem with this

man – whom she believed was a gentle, kind individual underneath – the trainer asked him bluntly: 'How do you function at work each day when you leave your heart at home?' After tearfully recounting his experiences in Vietnam, which had forced him to lock up his heart in order 'to do bad things to good people', this man – the senior vice-president of the company – agreed to apologise to his entire team for disrespecting them. Trust, collaboration, commitment and fun were undoubtedly built between them from that moment on.

~ Every journey starts with a single step ~

It is possible to achieve anything within the workplace as long as you are dedicated and committed to your goal. Consider how Richard Barrett, formerly an assistant to one of the vice-presidents at the World Bank in Washington, started the Spiritual Unfoldment Society (SUS). in which colleagues met to promote spiritual enlightenment in the workplace. From a small start, membership grew to around 400 individuals and SUS instituted monthly meditation sessions, set up an international conference to explore ethical and spiritual values in relation to sustainable development (sponsored by their employer, the World Bank) and regularly discussed ways to encourage higher consciousness and love at work. If Barrett, now an internationally acclaimed key-note speaker and author of *Liberating the Corporate Soul: A values-based approach to building visionary organisations*, could persuade conservative bank staff to bring their hearts and souls into work, couldn't you find it possible to inject some fun and lightness into the working day?

Finally, remember that the word enlightenment contains a vitally important syllable: light. As G K Chesterton once said: 'Angels fly because they take themselves lightly.' This is a useful quote to reflect on as we move into the next chapter on handling difficult working relationships.

AFFIRMATIONS

- ✔ I am opening up to the possibility that my work can be fun.
- ✔ I am committing myself to setting an example of fun, laughter and happiness in my workplace.
- ✔ I am appreciative of all the people in my life who bring me joy and pleasure.
- ✔ I am a hugely creative individual who is starting to recognise the value of play in that process.
- ✔ I am setting myself the goal of transforming my working life into one of fun from this moment on.
- ✔ I make no apologies for wishing to be a happychondriac.

✎ Your action list from this chapter

Write down at least six things that you intend to do now – ie, today not tomorrow – based on what you have learned in this chapter.

1

2

3

4

5

6

---

*"Playfulness is a forgotten language
that adults can easily relearn."*
Matt Weinstein, Managing to Have Fun

CHAPTER SEVEN

Are your working relationships making you unhappy?

"In the light of the most recent findings in physics
the fact is that no real division can be found between ourselves,
other people and the world around us – unless we create it in our minds."
George Land and Beth Jarman, *Breakpoint and Beyond*

Many of us have had the experience of buying our dream house or apartment – in the ideal location, at a perfect price, a place that's structurally sound and with room for scope in interior design, etc – only to find out that living there is a nightmare experience because of the neighbours. Similarly, a job you are passionate about can turn sour because your co-workers, boss or, if you're self-employed or freelance, your commissioning agents, are downright unpleasant or difficult.

Yet there is a technique that, once taken on board, will transform your interactions with others both inside and out-side the workplace. It will not eliminate your relationship problems overnight but will give you the capacity to welcome and benefit from, rather than avoid and fear, interpersonal clashes. This technique – and I don't underestimate how chal-lenging this can be – involves changing your mind about the nature of relationships, thinking about them in terms of cata-lysts that offer you a rewarding opportunity to grow mentally, emotionally and spiritually.

Nowhere are strong emotions more likely to be triggered than in our dealings with other people, and few things cause us more emotional distress than being the butt of someone's displeasure, anger, hatred or just downright intransigence. Yet the words emotion and motivation come from the same Latin root, *movere*. As author Frances Wilks says in her book *Intelligent Emotion*: 'Suffering brings us up short and opens us to the point of seeing things differently. When we suffer the depths of emotional distress, it makes us want to do something to end the pain.' The best possible choice we can make is to 'end the pain' constructively and positively, which is why a degree of mental adjustment about relationships is so vital. This won't make all your future relationships absolutely hunky dory – nor should it. Architects looking to strengthen a weak wall increase the load it has to bear, not lessen it, so causing the parts to fuse together more firmly. Similarly, (as you may remember from your childhood), when you have come through a relationship clash positively and 'made friends' again, you can share a level of love and camaraderie with that other person that didn't exist before. Tension is an essential part of mental well-being, in the same way that we require a certain amount of stress to motivate us to get out of bed in the morning. It is not equilibrium we need to strive for in our relationships but a way of giving meaning to the constant struggles and conflicts between people.

The importance of establishing positive relationships when you are working from the heart is not simply to enhance your experience but to ensure you remain employable. Organisations are looking to employ workers who are people-oriented, but in a more defined way than simply getting along with others. In addition to job-related skills, today's major corporations are now looking for individuals with the sort of interpersonal skills that make them ideal mentors, coaches, counsellors and informal supporters of others. It is no longer enough to be good at what you do within the working environment, you have to have the abilities and willingness to help others be better too.

The renowned Viennese psychiatrist Viktor Frankl outlines three main ways in which we can find meaning in life: through our work or the things we do, through the attitude required to turn tragedy into triumph, and through our experiences with other people. Remember the 'life as a classroom' analogy from Chapter 2? (See page 51.) Then think of the difficult people you meet as representing a series of challenging papers or exams, none of which will deflect you from graduating from that spiritual classroom with honours. These individuals have come into your life to help reveal your deficiencies (that is, where you lack interpersonal skills – you haven't done enough 'homework'), your intolerances, your preconceptions and assumptions and the degree to which you sabotage your-self through fearing success or failure. There are so many lessons to be learned from interacting with others that it is nigh on impossible to be prescriptive about how you should deal with a given situation. However, this chapter looks at three different kinds of attitude shift that can help. By adapting them to your needs you will find that coming face to face with difficult or challenging people no longer prevents you from fully benefiting from the work you love to do. These attitudes concern:

● How you see yourself: understanding that the quality of your relationship with yourself determines the quality of every other relationship you have because life reflects back to you who you think you are

● How you see others: learning to understand another person's version of 'reality' and welcoming conflicting views as an opportunity to broaden your own understanding of life

● How others see you: accepting that you need other people to help you reach your goals and that they may view you in a very different light to the way you view yourself.

Before we look more closely at these three kinds of attitude, and engage in some exercises to help you make the necessary mental adjustments to view your relationships in a more positive light, let's focus on the bigger picture for a moment; both in terms of the age-old belief in reincarnation and karma, and the new physics.

In *As You Like It*, William Shakespeare wrote, 'All the world's a stage, And all the men and women merely players,' referring to the 'seven ages' of man and the fact that we take on different parts or roles throughout our lives. Life as theatre is a valuable metaphor, one that can help us create a happier, more meaningful attitude in relation to those people who take on bit parts or major roles in our various 'soul dramas'. There is increasing evidence from respected therapists working in the field of hypnotic regression that supports the view that our soul needs to experience many lifetimes before achieving the goal of enlightenment. Belief in reincarnation – or at least an intellectual acceptance of its logic – offers a compelling explanation of why we are here. Just as in a repertory company a player may take on the role of Romeo one season and the second spear carrier in *Julius Caesar* in another, our soul family joins us incarnation after incarnation to help us play out certain karmic themes and experience the emotions which, as spirits, we have taken human form to encounter.

Viewing your life as a soul drama can help you see difficulties from a more objective perspective and help release your attachment to any individual reality, all of which is illusory anyway. Your current incarnation becomes easier to accept and understand when you realise that, throughout your many lives, you have been both male and female, black and white, victim and oppressor, rich and poor, healthy and diseased. Those we have tortured – mentally or physically – in a previous life will teach us what it is to experience torture in this one; while those who have been on the receiving end of our kindness and love today will show us what that feels like in a future incarnation. To free ourselves from the chains of the human ego as embodied by our current life is our ultimate goal and relationships are a valuable catalyst in that experience.

~ Energetic connections ~

We live in exciting times, when the ability to develop our potential as unique and somewhat chaotic individuals is being aided and encouraged by science through its greater understanding of how the mind and body works, both separately and together. It is from the rather unorthodox domain of quantum physics that we now find scientific explanations for principles and concepts that have been espoused for centuries by philosophers and spiritual teachers.

Ours is a world of paradox, where matter exists simultaneously as particles and waves: concrete physical matter and fields of invisible energy. Instead of adhering to a set of quantifiable physical laws, quantum physicists have demonstrated that atomic matter reacts according to the intention of the viewer. Scientists who expect matter to be organised as static particles can observe this effect, while exactly the same substance can appear in wave state by those who expect to observe waves. This suggests what many wise individuals have intuitively believed: that life is a self-fulfilling prophecy. As Henry Ford once said: 'Whether you believe you can, or whether you believe you can't – you're absolutely right.' Or, as contemporary US self-development guru Wayne Dyer puts it: 'When you believe it, you'll see it.'

From examining the subatomic world of waves and particles we can begin to understand the paradox of our reality: that we are both being and becoming at the same time. That is, we live in a visible, tangible world of 'being', or 'particles', while at the same time being constantly bathed in an invisible, intangible web of unexpressed potential: the 'becoming' of the wave state. Both are essential aspects of our lives. As will be discussed further in Chapter Nine, it's important not to be so busy 'becoming' – that is, creating in your mind the possibilities for your future happiness and fulfilment – that you forget to 'be' in the moment. Because in a tangible sense, each moment is all we have.

This is also invaluable advice for those of us who want to start working from the heart. Other people can sense when you are putting on an act. They may not be able to articulate what they feel is wrong, but probably can't shake off the sense that something about you isn't quite right. It's that feeling you get when someone has a wide grin but cold eyes; when you hear words that should be appealing but are spoken in a tone that is obviously insincere. Sometimes it's much more elusive and indescribable than that and the more sensitive among us can choose to tap into a deep-rooted, intuitive level which suggests that something is not quite right between ourselves and another person, even though we can't explain this in any logical sense.

The belief that we are separate from other people helps fuel interpersonal conflicts. Yet modern physics has demonstrated that we are all connected energetically to everything and everyone else. Medical science has long recognised the mechanical, electrical and chemical energy that allows our bodies to function properly, and measures it with electro-encephalograms, electro-cardiograms, magnetic resonance imaging and positron emission tomography. Advances in quantum physics have taken this concept even further by revealing that instead of being the impenetrable, 'billiard ball' that scientists once thought it was, atomic matter (which is what our bodies consist of) is actually 99.9999 per cent empty space filled with energy. The reason why we experience matter as solid is thought to be due to a combination of the force of gravity and the way our brains are hard-wired. We are energetic beings, bundles of vibrating energy, a concept we commonly express through our language. Today, not only New Age converts use language like 'That resonates with me', 'I picked up bad vibes from that place', 'He wasn't on my wavelength', 'She energises me'.

Alternative approaches to healthcare such as homoeopathy, Bach flower remedies, spiritual healing and Reiki are explained in terms of an invisible, healing energy force that can pass from a herb, plant or person to rebalance and harmonise the dysfunctional frequencies in our bodies that produce disease. Healers working with crystals, chakras, Kirlian photography and auras talk about a bio-electromagnetic field that radiates through and around all things, which has been depicted as a halo around the heads and bodies of spiritual individuals in religious paintings. Experts in the new field of 'energy medicine' believe that this energy field is like a magnetic tape, containing information about an individual's physical, mental, spiritual and emotional state. As such, it can help predict diseases before they have a physical impact and may well transform how we perceive preventative medicine in the future. In *The Celestine Prophecy,* James Redfield talks about 'energy givers' and 'energy takers' – people with whom you feel energised, vibrant and alive in contrast to those who drain you emotionally and physically like spiritual vampires.

It is through an appreciation of the energetic connection between people that we can suggest why some relationships are harmonious while others are not. The reason why some people we immediately connect and have an empathy with, while others we take an instant dislike to for no logical reason can be explained using the analogy of a tuning fork. When such an instrument is sounded near a piano, for example, all the notes with the same resonance vibrate while the others remain unaffected. Similarly, it is thought that people who share the same energetic frequency are drawn to each other and interact positively, while those whose energies are disharmonious are deeply suspicious or may even actively dislike one another on sight. Yet because we need tension and challenge to motivate us to grow and develop, it is the disharmonious relationships that can sometimes be the most rewarding and valuable to us, causing us to confront how we see ourselves, the rest of humanity and the relationship between the two. Once we can embrace the idea that difficult people are the catalysts for our spiritual growth then we can start to look forward to – and be grateful for – the challenges presented by them, rather than avoid them.

In a world comprising nothing but energy, the division between people is only a perceptual one, involving different vibrational rates. Therefore, you are intimately linked with every person who exists now or who has ever lived; there is no need to feel separate or isolated – or different.

"Pay careful attention to what pushes people's mental buttons. If you can push those buttons for the better, do it."
Scott Adams,
Cartoonist and creator of 'Dilbert'

~ How you see yourself ~

In Chapter Two we looked at our subconscious dark side, Jung's 'shadow side' and the fact that we project those bits of ourselves we dislike most on to other people. Before we explore this concept further, try the following exercise.

✎ Exercise: Dear me

Take a sheet of paper and write a letter, headed 'Dear XXX,' addressing it to someone at work whom you dislike intensely, someone who has hurt or offended you in the past or with whom you are experiencing some difficulty in a relationship.

Be completely honest about your feelings in this letter, don't hold anything back. You don't need to be concerned about justifying yourself or making your objections rational; just let the words flow.

Once you have completed your letter, go back to the heading and change the name of the other person to your own. Now read that letter again and think about how your accusations might reveal a message from your inner self about those parts of you that you prefer to repress and ignore.

To what extent does this give you a new perspective on your relationship with yourself, and the other person? Do you feel comfortable dishonouring someone else when you are 'guilty' of the same sort of behaviour, albeit in a different context? For example, you might find that drivers who 'cut you up' make you apoplectic with rage. And, of course, you never do that yourself – not on the road, anyway. But can you think of an occasion when, in your haste to get to where you want to go in your career, you have thoughtlessly ridden roughshod over someone else?

Part of the human condition is to want to lay the blame on others for our unhappiness. But the more we can accept that our discomfort lies in the fact that there are parts of ourselves we neither like nor wish to acknowledge, the more accepting we will be of other people's shortcomings and stop expecting them to make us feel better about ourselves. In the same way that experiencing a serious illness, unemployment, the loss of a child, or rejection by your lover broadens your understanding of what these have meant to other people – and in doing so makes you stronger, wiser and more compassionate – facing and owning your shadow side means that you increase your self-love, which, in turn, increases your capacity to love other people. It also dissipates fear since instead of always running away from your internal dragon you learn to jump on its back and ride it.

Today, think about the one person with whom you are having greatest difficulties, particularly in relation to your work; someone who causes you a welter of negative emotions like fear, anger, hatred, envy or aggression. Think seriously about how their behaviour and attributes mirror what's going on inside you.

My friend Susie was very hurt by a business colleague who suddenly went cold on her after enthusing about all the ways they could work together on various creative projects. It was only after talking this through for a while that Susie realised she has a tendency to cold-shoulder people she has formerly been very warm towards because it's the way she deals with pressure. By side-lining others and conveniently forgetting about her relationships, Susie could then focus on her work without guilt or interruptions. She never realised what an impact this had on the other person until she experienced similar treatment herself.

The magical thing about relationships is that simply by changing your attitude towards yourself you change the dynamics of every other relationship you have. That in turn has an effect on the other person. Once you can own your inner anger, angry people become less intimidating. By looking upon relationship problems as a genuine attempt to learn more about yourself – and then accepting that you have a shadow side as well as many good points – you can come to terms with human failings by simply 'being' and not 'doing'. Dostoevsky articulates this concept elegantly in *The Brothers Karamazov* when he writes: 'Avoid a feeling of aversion towards others and towards yourself: what seems to you bad in yourself is purified by the very fact that you've noticed it.'

~ **How you see others** ~

Most of us have a tendency to think the whole world sees things the same way that we do – and it can come as an almighty shock to find out that it doesn't. While you may find another person's point of view totally alien to your own, remember the words of Voltaire, who said: 'I disapprove of what you say, but I will defend to the death your right to say it.' It is only by acknowledging and accepting the differences between us that we broaden and enrich our own experience of life. Being able to take a multiple perspective, particularly when you're at loggerheads with someone else, allows you the sort of flexible response common to successful individuals.

The following exercise has been cloned from a personal development approach called Neuro Linguistic Programming (NLP), which, to sum up this broad discipline as briefly as possible, is the study of the structure of subjective experience and in particular the study of excellence. At the heart of NLP is the principle of respecting another person's model of the world or view of reality. Out of this has developed a technique called perceptual positions, which is invaluable in helping you see life from someone else's point of view.

Exercise: Perceptual positions

Think of an interpersonal conflict which you are experiencing, or which you have faced in the past and remains unresolved.

1 Close your eyes, relax and take the 'first position' by being aware of your thoughts and how you feel about the situation. Try to give these thoughts and feelings a shape, or a colour, perhaps imagining them as an animal or bird.

Now imagine there's an empty box by your side into which you place those representations of your anger, hurt, annoyance, irritation; whatever it is you are feeling. Try to empty your mind and body of all the negativity you are holding on to and associate with this situation.

2 Now take the 'second position'. Imagine what this situation might look or feel like from the other person's point of view.

Try to get a handle on what it's like to be inside that other person's mind and what issues might be connected with this conflict from their perspective. Do you sense a certain amount of fear, for example? Again, give it a colour or shape or some other tangible connection. When you think you have a handle on the thoughts and feelings of the person you are facing challenges with, release them all into the box beside you.

3 Now take the 'third position', which involves detaching yourself from either your point of view or theirs, and being as objective as you can about the situation. How does the relationship and the issues surrounding it look from this perspective? Take your time to assess how this conflict might appear to a complete outsider and what their perspective might be on it. Once again, release these thoughts and feelings into the box and bring yourself back into the present.

After you have practised this technique in a meditative way for a while you will find that you can take a second or third position on potentially combative situations at the time the dispute is happening. This will help you not only become more understanding of the differences between people but will assist you in reaching a mutually acceptable compromise.

~ How others see you ~

The following exercise is a technique that will help you think about the extent to which others see you differently to the way you see yourself. No matter how self-sufficient or self-managing we like to think of ourselves, somewhere down the line we will need the assistance and co-operation of other people, therefore effective interpersonal skills are vital at work. If you are at loggerheads with the accounts clerk who looks after your invoices or expenses or tend to – albeit unwittingly – put the back up of your company's IT specialists who are there to help you sort out your computer problems, or just come over as brash and overconfident to people who might otherwise want to engage your services, this will inevitably hinder your ability to reach your goals. This is the case whether you consider their attitudes towards you to be fair or not.

✎ Exercise: Seeing yourself as others see you

The following list of adjectives could refer to your life both inside and outside of work. Go through the list and circle the six adjectives that you think best describe you. As always, there are no right or wrong answers, but you will get the greatest benefits if you accept the six adjectives that most draw your attention. Don't spend too long mulling over what others might think or what is socially acceptable.

Adaptable	Individualistic	Trusting
Honest	Supportive	Sharing
Fair	Extrovert	Nurturing
Professional	Imaginative	Honourable
Friendly	Prepared	Objective
Realistic	Cautious	Tough
Consistent	Determined	Open
Self-confident	Knowledgeable	Practical

Now look at your list and try to identify the common themes between these adjectives. Once you have identified the theme, try to name it. What does it say about you? The following are a few examples that people often report together. Of course, your list will probably be entirely different; remember that everyone is unique.

> self-confident, extrovert and determined
> honest, trusting and honourable
> adaptable, friendly and supportive

Now take a second look at your list. In trying to understand the implication of these aptitudes on your ability to reach your goals, is there even a remote possibility that some others may see you in a different light?

On the next page are some examples of the opposites to your strengths. On first reading of the list, you may feel that they do not apply to you, but try to step back and think about them objectively. Perhaps you could ask a trusted friend for an opinion.

Adaptable	=	unfocused
Individualistic	=	separatist
Trusting	=	gullible
Honest	=	tactless
Supportive	=	submissive
Loyal	=	servile
Fair	=	indecisive
Extrovert	=	forceful or aggressive
Nurturing	=	smothering
Professional	=	too formal
Imaginative	=	unrealistic/a day-dreamer
Honourable	=	moralistic
Friendly	=	indiscriminate
Prepared	=	lacking in spontaneity
Objective	=	unexpressive/lacking passion
Realistic	=	pessimistic
Cautious	=	unambitious
Tough	=	uncaring
Consistent	=	inflexible
Determined	=	over-ambitious
Open	=	indiscreet
Self-confident	=	arrogant
Knowledgeable	=	a 'know-it-all'
Practical	=	unimaginative

To bring all the work together that you have already done on understanding yourself, look back at your list of personal goals on page 18. How does the way you see yourself compared to how others might see you (ie, the six adjectives and their potential downsides) have an impact on your personal goals? For example, if your main goal is for affection, and you value honesty, do your friends ever think of you as a little *too* honest, ie, occasionally tactless? If your goal is to be an expert on a special subject and you feel it is important to be knowledgeable, do other people perceive you on occasions as a know-it-all? If you strive to be a good leader and have confidence in your ability, might there be occasions when the people you work with could think you are arrogant? If you are determined to become wealthy, do those around you think of you as over-ambitious?

~ The importance of communication ~

No matter how much we might decry unexplained phenomena, most of us seem to have great confidence in ESP (extra sensory perception). Why else would we expect other people to know what we think and feel, without bothering to tell them? How often have you maintained bad feelings towards a co-worker or partner because they haven't done something you expected them to – even though you didn't explain what you wanted in the first place? Yet why should people automatically know what's going on inside your head? Can you say that you accurately know what's going on inside the heads of other people? If you do then that's a very rare talent indeed.

Think back to the last relationship problem you had and the extent to which you calmly communicated your feelings and needs to that other person. Let me demonstrate the sort of difficulties that can arise when two people fail to communicate with each other.

Cathryn and Jenna were asked to collaborate on a book. Neither of them knew each other and were so focused on the task (that is, writing the book to a very tight deadline) that they never considered the need to talk about their individual styles of working. Within a very short time some major differences in how each saw their 'reality' began to impact the speed and effectiveness of their collaboration. Cathryn expected to do her day job during the week and work on the book at weekends only. She believed it was Jenna's responsibility to do most of the research (they hadn't discussed who was responsible for that, either), cancelled meetings at the last minute because of other commitments and sent material to Jenna on a sporadic basis. Jenna, who was much more ordered in her approach, expected Cathryn to have set aside the next three months to write the book together, as she had done. She objected to what she perceived to be Cathryn's overbearing attitude and became increasingly unhappy when deadlines were missed. Neither woman talked to each other about their concerns but expected the other to work in a similar way to herself. The result was a book that not only failed to meet its deadline date with the publisher but which had to be considerably re-written. Both were so task focused that they forgot the cardinal rule for effective team working: put the relationship first; get to know who you are working with.

A lot can be learned from theatrical techniques when it comes to bringing people together to achieve a specific task. For example, a theatre director will devote a whole week of six weeks' rehearsal time to ensure an ensemble of players develops rapport, trust and a spirit of co-operation before asking them to read and rehearse the script. Business rarely writes in that sort of time factor, throwing people together on projects and expecting them to gel together as well as do a good job. Most projects, mergers and acquisitions fail because of problems with people, not skills, usually because of a perceived – and undiscussed – incompatibility between ways of working, culture and methods of integration.

Working with others is as intense and challenging as any marriage. Yet how often do we metaphorically go on a 'date' with our co-workers before being thrown together in an uncomfortable liaison for the lengths of time our partners rarely enjoy from us? No wonder there are so many corporate equivalents of divorce. Getting to know someone beyond the skills they are bringing to a job or project ensures that when challenges crop up – as they inevitably do – you have already developed a rapport which encourages openness, honesty and bonding. This then allows both parties to find a way – and want to find a way – to compromise and reach agreement. The alternative is low morale, greater stress resulting in sickness absence, increased staff turnover and reduced productivity. That's not only a sorry situation for workers to be in but it doesn't make good business sense either.

~ James's story ~

Jumping precipitously from one job to another without recognising what is really important to you may boost your bank balance but deplete your heart and soul, as James discovered.

When word got round that the management consultancy arm of the company he worked for was in danger of being radically pruned, James immediately decided to jump ship and started sending out his résumé. Within weeks he was offered the position of human resources director in a multinational corporation, with an increased salary and many company benefits, working in plush new offices in a prestigious part of the city.

Almost from day one, James was unhappy there. He discovered that his department was staffed by ineffectual and uncommitted individuals who resented his desire to upgrade the way HR was viewed by the rest of the company. They'd been happy to be administrators and paper-pushers for many years and were out of rhythm with James's view of HR's counselling and career-development role. After a lot of unpleasantness and struggle, James was finally able to staff the department with professionals like himself, with a passion for putting people first.

However, his 'people problems' were only beginning. A clash of personalities between James and the company's sales and marketing director contributed to the fact that their weekly meetings resembled a school playground. The managing director and the sales director, who frequently met socially and whose wives were close friends, joined forces against James, making no effort to hide the fact that they had arranged behind his back to veto any suggestions for improving the status of human resources. The problem was that the divisional managers had been operating their departments autonomously for so long that they wanted to continue to hire and fire at will, without any reference to HR. With no cohesive policy on recruiting or redeployment, James recognised that the company was not only frequently morally wrong in its handling of redundancies and sackings, but could be risking future legal difficulties. Feeling completely cut off and unsupported, James gave up his crusade for the sake of his health, kept his head down and was almost relieved when he heard he was being made redundant in the next raft of job cuts.

With no idea of what to do next, James was approached by another headhunter who suggested he head up a charitable foundation which needed a clear-sighted, energetic visionary to take it into the new millennium. James knew this body by reputation and was not impressed: it was largely ineffectual, with little funding and an out-dated image. The job also came with a substantial drop in salary and few perks. Not sure why he agreed to do so, except that it seemed to be the right thing, James agreed to meet the team in their dingy offices.

His attitude changed the moment he was greeted by the bright, passionate, committed individuals who worked there. Afterwards he summed up his decision to take on the job in four words: 'I love the people.' Ironically, for someone who had always worked in people management, James only then realised that good working relationships are his *sine qua non*; that he could take on any challenge, accept a lower salary, be in an aesthetically challenging working environment yet be happy if the people he was surrounded with loved and supported one another.

The chairman of the charity, whom James warmed to immediately, recognising in him an invaluable mentor, agreed to compensate James's lower salary by giving him self-employed status so he could take on lucrative consultancy work on the side.

Some months later, James was having a drink with a friend. The friend used a big advertising agency which had just been taken over, and he had withdrawn his account as a result. When asked why he had done that, the friend replied: 'Because I was buying more than creativity and service, which I could get from any good agency. What I was really buying into were relationships and understanding.'

For the first time James understood what he meant.

"If you want more satisfaction from your work,
you have to negotiate better relationships
with the people you work with."
Deborah Lee, author and social psychologist

~ Communications checklist ~

Here are some suggestions for improving the way you communicate with others that are consistent with taking your
heart and soul into work. They will not only help you enhance
your relationships, but will also contribute to greater happiness and fulfilment at work.

- Accept that it is your responsibility to communicate your
  intentions, expectations and needs to others before you
  begin a project or task.
- Allow for the fact that another person may have different
  needs, objectives and problems to your own. Find out
  what they want to achieve, compare this with what you
  want to achieve and then try to find a solution where
  both sides win.
- Allow others to maintain their self-esteem by depersonal-
  ising your comments or criticisms. Instead of saying,
  'Your lateness is unprofessional', try substituting: 'I find
  your being late makes it difficult for me to be as efficient
  as I want to be.'
- Ask questions and listen to the other person's point of
  view before rushing in to attack them or defend your
  own position. Communication is as much about active
  listening as influential verbal skills.
- Take the time to meet your co-workers informally and
  establish a rapport with them by finding common areas
  of interest aside from work.
- Remember that anyone you are communicating with is a
  person, not just a job title.
- Find someone you consider to be an effective, well-
  respected and caring communicator and study (by asking
  them if necessary) how they do that.
- Practise communicating with people outside your own
  immediate team or department. Get out of the habit of
  only dealing with like-minded individuals.
- Look first for the good in every person you meet. Find
  what they do right – and tell them – and not just what
  they do wrong.

- Remember that while you may be speaking through your mouth your soul communicates through the eyes; maintain eye contact.
- Modulate your vocal pace and tone of voice in line with the person you are speaking with. No matter how much someone might agree with what you have to say, your message will be lost if you are rattling it off at high speed to someone with naturally slow speech.
- When it comes to getting your point across, quality is better than quantity.
- In study after study, honesty is the one value that individuals say they seek and admire most in others, particularly at work. They also admit how rare it is to find it. Practise having open and honest, but tactful, exchanges with everyone you meet. The more you do this the easier and more comfortable it gets.
- You might not need thanks or praise from others but that doesn't mean everyone feels the same. A thank you for a job well done or even a quick 'Hello, how are you today?' can mean the difference between a good or bad day for someone.
- People bond with others who are prepared to share ideas, thoughts and opinions. It's this bonding that helps avoid and heal otherwise potentially damaging relationship conflicts.
- Whenever you are in conflict with someone, stick to the facts. If you don't know the full story – ask.
- No matter how angry you are with someone, never get personal and descend to name calling or character assassination.
- Are you seen as the person who communicates good news but prefers to leave the bad news to someone else?
- Avoid the tendency to say nothing in conversation then moan to others that you aren't being heard.
- Ask yourself if you are against someone else's solution to a problem, or ideas, because it isn't a good one – or because it is different from your own.
- Always be cheerful, enthusiastic and positive.

~ Case study: British Airways ~ and Careerlink

Careerlink was set up by British Airways Human Resources in November 1996 to provide guidance and advice to line management, and a range of redeployment and outplacement services to the estimated 5,000 staff who would be changing jobs or leaving the airline as part of the company's £1 billion Business Efficiency Programme.

BA recognised that the attitude and approach of its employees are directly linked to the company's ability to remain competitive. It has therefore focused one of its goals on developing 'Inspired People': individuals with the innate interpersonal skills of communication, leadership, self-motivation and service to others. The role of Careerlink is fundamental to the achievement of that goal.

Many of the techniques used by Careerlink's team of experienced advisors are consistent with those found in this book. Clients seeking career moves are helped to understand what things are important to them and where they can add value, self-worth being an important motivator.

British Airways is one example of a company recognising that people are at the heart of its business and that it is vital to find employees who bring themselves to the job, regardless of whether they are in the front line or not. As Careerlink's manager, Rowena Davies, explains:

'The front-line customer service is just the tip of the iceberg. Many staff behind the scenes never meet the travelling public but BA expects all its staff to be customer oriented because "customers" are internal as well as external.

'You may be a clerical assistant, an engineer or an analyst, but how you assist an individual in another part of the business can ultimately affect how the customer is greeted by the check-in, telesales or cargo agent, never forgetting that the customer then has the choice of whether to do business with BA again. We explain to people that you may never meet the customer in your working life but that how you operate, the style in which you communicate and the relationship you have with your colleagues is critical to the success of the business.'

Hence BA is looking for the sort of individuals who bring more than job-related skills to their work: they bring their hearts, and a belief that what they have to contribute is important and valued.

Now we look at one of the greatest challenges most people face in today's hectic world: the importance of maintaining a balanced life.

AFFIRMATIONS

- ✔ I am committing myself daily to improving my relationships with others.
- ✔ I am opening myself up daily to new perspectives by honouring the differences in others.
- ✔ I am strengthening my energetic connection with everyone I meet.
- ✔ I am starting to recognise that the things I hate most about others I repress in myself.
- ✔ There is no right or wrong, just different ways of looking at the world.

✍ Your action list from this chapter

Write down at least six things that you intend to do now – ie, today not tomorrow – based on what you have learned in this chapter.

1

2

3

4

5

6

CHAPTER EIGHT

Are your work and the rest of your life in balance?

"There's no such thing as work-life balance if you can't get enough
of both work and life."
Robert B Reich, former United States Secretary of Labor

The following list was sent to me recently by e-mail. It was meant to be a joke but some of the points were uncomfortably familiar.

You know you're work-obsessed when ...

- You communicate with your family by e-mail
- You fax your Christmas list to your parents
- Your dining-room table becomes an extension of your desk
- You know it's the weekend because that's when you wear casual clothes to work
- You talk to people socially with phrases like 'progressing action plans', 'calendarising projects' and 'thinking out of the box'
- You recognise staff at airport hotels more easily than you do your next-door neighbours
- Your home is decorated with multitudinous Post-it notes
- Your chat-up lines include references to the best business books you've read
- You've forgotten where the supermarket is, let alone how to cook
- You lecture your kids on the importance of time management for doing their homework (and, if they dare to ask you to help, the importance of being self-motivated and self-managed in today's environment).

Balance has become the buzzword of the 1990s, ironically at a time when workaholism remains rife. Contemporary dictionaries have even noted the introduction of a new word into the English language. Presenteeism, coined originally by Professor Cary Cooper, describes the activity of individuals who work long hours even when there's little or nothing to do, for fear of losing their jobs. They are being encouraged by employers who demand commitment but would sack them tomorrow if corporate pragmatism demanded it. Presenteeism is fear-based behaviour and what this book has hopefully done for you so far is demonstrate that employability – and hence your future security – comes from working from the heart. When you are focused on a compelling goal, have high self-esteem, constantly re-appraise your skills set and learn new ones as appropriate, when you know how to read life's signs, see the bigger picture, understand the reason for challenges and trust that you will succeed in whatever you set your mind to, then you recognise that presenteeism is a mug's game that holds no appeal for you.

Workaholism, on the other hand, commonly masks not just fear but also hints at unmet emotional and spiritual needs, typified by the man who works long hours because he no longer loves his partner and hopes she'll let him off the hook by being the one to walk away. Or women like Anne (see page 44) who use work as an excuse for not confronting their soul's despair.

However, many people argue that if you are working on something you feel passionate about then you'll become even more of a workaholic than before. The vision of the passion-driven workaholic is largely a myth. In a 1998 survey by the UK Institute of Personnel and Development, only 7 per cent of those polled said they worked extra hours because they enjoyed their work. For many respondents, work squeezed out their home life because their workload and the pressures of the job required it. The fact that the 'great majority of workers believe they have the right balance between home and work' is either a cause for celebration or concern that perhaps we have just got used to making our home lives second best.

In another survey, one-fifth of 1,100 managers questioned said if they had to choose, they would put their career before their personal life, and another fifth said they might consider it. This from a sample of people routinely working six days a week for more than 51 hours.

Working from the heart does not equate to work addiction because it recognises that to take a whole person to work you have to be a whole person with a life that's rich and varied.

Let's look at what will probably happen to many of those managers who put their work before their home life in this modern fairy story of a typical workaholic we'll call David. (Sorry to appear sexist here but all the statistics suggest that men work longer hours than women.)

David has a well-paid executive position with lots of perks. He travels, stays in good hotels and enjoys expense account lunches. He's been married a long time and, because he's never been there much for his children, subconsciously protects himself by being a distant parent. David thinks his wife doesn't understand or is not interested in what he does; she's just happy to spend his money. He's had a few affairs over the years because their sex life is not what it was. Boy, is he glad to get out of the house just to be free of all that nagging, the cold-shoulders, the noise and the demands of kids who don't seem to realise they couldn't have all that fancy computer equipment if Daddy didn't work so hard.

Then one day, out of the blue, the axe falls and David is out of a job. He becomes depressed: he gave that company the best years of his life, dammit, and this is all the thanks he gets. He either turns to his wife for support because he so desperately needs someone to make him feel like a worthwhile person again, or he takes his anger out on her. After years of neglect she is antagonised by either behaviour; she realises she's had enough of him and leaves, taking the children. In her eyes, all that had been left for her in the latter years of their marriage was financial security, and now that's gone there is nothing more to stay for.

David's ex-colleagues – many of whom he regarded as friends, his only friends come to think of it – are too embarrassed to speak to him. He would like to go out for a drink to drown his sorrows only he has no one to go with. The days drag on because there is no status, recreation, intimacy or just something to do any more. The money is dwindling fast because they'd always lived well beyond their means and now his wife is demanding her fair share of what's left. Life seems to be on a downward spiral and all David can think about is how quickly he can get another job.

See what happens when your life revolves around a single focus, work? When that focus is taken away through redundancy, retirement, ill health, or any other reason, your 'box' is empty. But the more you fill your life with activities that are of equal importance to you, then even if several of them disappear temporarily or permanently, you have enough resources to still view life as meaningful and rich.

✍ Exercise: The power of nine

Take a large sheet of paper (minimum size A4) and divide it into nine equal squares. Label each square with one of nine areas that to you represent a well-balanced life; the one that you ideally would like to live. The following is simply a list of suggestions. Head up your boxes however you choose.

- Romance/intimacy
- Family
- Friends
- Career/life purpose
- Spiritual growth/personal development
- Health
- Money
- Hobbies
- Fun/recreation
- Creativity
- Community service
- 'Me' time
- Educational activities
- Travel
- Physical environment (house, garden)
- Practical tasks

Now buy a packet of small coloured stickers (circles or squares), each sticker to represent a four-hour time slot. Starting on a Monday morning, make a note of how you currently allocate your time to each of these desired areas in your life and attach the appropriate number of stickers. Do this for at least a week. Then review just how balanced your life is. Which areas need more attention? Are you taking on too many work commitments or practical tasks at the expense of 'Me' time or creativity? To what extent does work dominate your life and are you really happy with that proportion? In what ways might this imbalance affect you in the future?

"Some of those who work long hours feel that they have things under control, they have chosen their present balance between home and work and are content with it. It's not the hours as such that matter, but the sense of having got the balance right."
Mike Emmott, IPD policy advisor

Be aware that achieving sustained balance in your life must be underpinned by passion and commitment. Most New Year's resolutions fail because they relate to things you believe you *should* do rather than really *want* to, so try to ensure that your 'life box' is filled with activities that bring you joy. That means looking for the positive rather than the negative benefit. Dieters motivated by negative thinking such as 'I want to stop being fat' or 'I want to not have to wear a size 16 any more' are focusing on what they don't want, which, ironically, they attract into their lives. The more empowering and therefore successful mindset would be: 'I want to be thinner' or 'I intend to be a size 12 in order to get into a slinky black dress by next Christmas'. With that in mind, come up with three objectives for each of your nine areas of balance. Make these goals SMART, which, in my version of this acronym, means:

- **Specific**: Fill in as much detail as you can about your chosen goal: that is, not that you are going to learn Spanish, but that you are going to learn conversational or business Spanish and for what purpose.
- **Motivational**: In the same way that most of us make New Year's resolutions that fail because we simply aren't that

fired up to achieve them, only settle on goals that you really want to achieve. Knowing why (as in the specifics, above) is an important detail here. Check your chosen goals against your Heartwork Plan. Do they really reflect who you are and what you want out of life? If they do, give yourself extra motivation by planning a reward for yourself when you have achieved them.

- **Achievable**: This again links with the previous point; if you set yourself an unrealistic goal then you are likely to become demotivated when you look unlikely to achieve it, for whatever reason. If you have never taken a singing lesson in your life and your only experience is warbling in the shower, it hardly makes sense to set yourself the goal of playing the lead in the local operatic society's next production. In the same way that you would set about eating a big piece of meat by cutting it into smaller chunks that you chew morsel by morsel, break each objective down into smaller tasks and tackle each one of those at a time.

- **Rateable**: Make sure you will know when you have achieved your objective, not just practically but also emotionally. What will it feel like to have accomplished this particular objective? If you can't get excited at the thought, are you really going to be that motivated when you come to do it?

- **Time framed**: Set yourself a deadline by which you will have met each of your three objectives: say, the first in a month, the second in three to six months and the third in a year. That way you will always have something to focus on in each of these areas, requiring different levels of attention and achievement.

"I realised that a ten per cent difference in how much I did was not the difference between success and failure."
David Nadler,
management consultant, Delta Consulting Group

~ Living with trade-offs ~

One of Stephen Covey's 'Seven Habits of Highly Effective People' is 'start with the end in mind'. In order to achieve and maintain a balanced life it is important to sense how that life will be, which means visualising it as vividly as possible. Then, when you have a compelling outcome to focus on, you can work backwards and break that goal down into small, incremental steps. However, in order to be a balanced individual you have many goals and it may be that some of them are in direct contradiction to the others.

Dreams are invaluable motivators. Every day I dream of the time when I'll spend a third of the year writing in sunny California, a third travelling in other parts of the world teaching and accumulating knowledge, and a third working out of the UK. It is this dream that really fires me up. However, when I eventually live across several continents my attachment to certain things will have to change. My possessions are all things I'm deeply proud of owning and love having around me but some will have to be sacrificed in order to allow my biggest dream to be fulfilled. Because of that I will have to decide what is most important to me: an itinerant lifestyle or lots of possessions in glorious surroundings in England?

Go through all the permutations of your dreams, just as you did with the Future Goals exercise (see pages 103–5), comparing one with another until you have reached a hierarchy that reflects which are the most important to you. If you had to choose between taking that dream job as a travel writer and spending more time at home with your family, what would it be? If you decided that your family is more important, think how you could do something about your other dream in the meantime, perhaps by specialising in travel articles about your local area for foreign press or magazines, or deciding to write a limited number of travel articles every year which fit with times that you can take the family with you.

Sometimes dreams are compatible, sometimes they're not. Sometimes they involve making difficult choices, communicating and asking others for help, or reviewing your time frames. That's just the way life is. Like children in a toy or sweet shop we have many wants and inevitably desire them all. Having to make choices challenges us to decide what is really important in our lives and encourages us to become more creative in finding a compromise. For example, suppose one of your dreams is to earn a much higher salary in order to finance a particular hobby or lifestyle, and another is to change your job to one involving greater risk and uncertainty but with the benefit of enhanced creative expression and ful-filment? Just as you were planning to hand in your notice you arc offered a huge salary increase to stay. Your first dream could be met immediately, but how long will that sustain you when your second dream is tugging at your heart-strings? Only you can answer that, and I would suggest you review the points made in Chapter Five on your relationship between money and work before you come to a conclusion.

The solution to such a dilemma doesn't always have to be black and white. In the above scenario you might ask yourself what you could do today – right now – to introduce greater creativity and fulfilment into your work. You could decide to dedicate yourself to the higher-paid work for, say, five years, all the time saving to reduce the risk of your dream job when you eventually embark on it. Scenario planning makes good sense both commercially and emotionally. It means benefiting from that wonderful internal mechanism you have to review your future life: your imagination. If you want to defeat the procrastination that comes from dreaming up a vision of the future with facets that, in reality, don't really fit together too well, then the time you invest now making choices and com-ing up with creative solutions to less-than-ideal scenarios will be well spent.

~ Balancing your time ~

This was never meant to be a chapter on time management, partly because there are numerous excellent books, courses and products available to help you work smarter that spend more time on that subject than is available here. But also because the term time management is a misnomer; what we're really talking about here is self-management. For all the list making and other principles, tools and techniques that such books can teach you, none will do any good unless you act on them. Which usually means thinking less about what you have to do and just getting on and doing it. Incomplete activities simply drain the creative energy that you could use more productively in another way.

If a thing requires action (and not everything does, so don't get caught up in unproductive busyness), get into the habit of employing one of the 3 Ds: Do it, Delegate it, or Defer it – but in a specific time-frame, preferably the same day or week. Obviously you may have to defer something because you don't have all the information you need to complete the task, but make sure you specify what follow-up action you need to take to clear 'deferrals' as quickly as possible. Stop fire-fighting and become more focused and organised about your work. Then you will undoubtedly find that time is not the enemy you thought it was, after all.

Working from the heart means recognising the need for balance in your life, no matter how much you love what you do for a living. Balance allows us to appreciate different perspectives about ourselves and how they contribute towards the whole.

Balanced living ensures we regularly relax our minds and bodies so that we come to work less stressed, more creative, more fun loving, more alive. And because of this we are invariably more effective and productive co-workers and employees, which tips the balance in our favour when jobs are being axed. Balance means recognising that we are not our jobs, but that each one of us is a complex, multi-faceted, unique individual with something special to offer the world. Embrace the notion of balance in your life and you will be in a stronger position to cope with change and uncertainty, you will always have the human support structure that is so psychologically vital to cope with life's failures and disappointments, and will maintain those precious commodities so many of us take for granted – including love and good health.

"There must be more to life than
having everything."
Maurice Sendak

~ Eileen's story ~

Eileen was a workaholic who has rebuilt her life after its foundations were shaken to the core, having not recognised the cracks early on.

This award-winning entrepreneur, key-note speaker and subject of a TV documentary on business millionaires started life as a coal miner's daughter on a bleak council estate in Coventry, England. Presented with limited career options as a teenager, Eileen went into nursing but her heart was never in it. Desperate to widen her life experience, Eileen moved to London, where she worked at a photographic studio and became interested in applying the models' make-up. From this small beginning in the beauty industry, Eileen came to realise that she was more interested in the therapy side and she began managing a skin clinic in London's Harley Street. During this time she came into contact with the US medical manufacturer of a facial toning machine which Eileen recognised would revolutionise beauty therapy. Out of a job when the clinic's directors went out of business, she leapt at the chance to act as the company's UK distributor.

Eileen started her business in 1991 with two other investors and within six years owned five premises, including a treatment clinic in Hampstead, London. Loving her job and – because of her own therapy background – remaining a very hands-on boss, Eileen worked long hours. The physical toll of this was exacerbated mentally by problems with the other directors, stemming from the fact that she had ended her live-in relationship with one of them. Eileen began to feel very isolated and unsupported.

While a great deal of internal wrangling was going on, Eileen suddenly found that she needed major spinal surgery for two slipped disks that were lying very close to a nerve. Before the operation she had to lie flat out for six weeks, and afterwards she endured a long period of convalescence. During this time of enforced reflection, all the emotional stuff that Eileen hadn't chosen to deal with in the previous twelve months came flooding out. She came to realise that letting go of her business was not such a big deal after all, as it wasn't what she had accomplished but who she was that mattered.

Instead of thinking of what she was losing, Eileen reviewed her experience in terms of what she had gained.

As her health improved, Eileen realised that the easiest thing would be to get back on the treadmill, perhaps starting up another business from scratch. After all, she had done it before. However, she decided to reflect on her life for a little longer after the shock of realising that her heart had not been in her company for a long time.

It was during this period, when she was both physically and emotionally vulnerable, that Eileen discovered how out of balance her life had become. While, in theory, she joined the chorus of people who say that no pay cheque compensates you for your health, Eileen had in fact been prepared to sacrifice this precious commodity on the altar of career success and financial gain.

Unable to look after herself during her convalescence, Eileen also discovered the extent to which she had shut out her family. Her mother came to look after her for six weeks, the first time in years that the two of them had shared a mother-daughter relationship. They talked in a way they had never done before.

Today, Eileen is a successful life coach who stresses the importance of balancing work with the rest of your life. She consciously makes her health a priority by regularly attending exercise classes, particularly Pilates. She also looks after her spiritual welfare with periods of meditation and finds her body and mind both benefit from slowing down and relaxing, as well as having fun and enjoying new relationships.

Work will always be an important part of Eileen's life but no more than all the other invaluable areas she has now rediscovered.

Now, as we turn to the final chapter, we look at a more profound kind of balance – the delicate balance between doing and being.

AFFIRMATIONS

✔ I am moving towards a more balanced life every day.

✔ My life is filling up with many compelling interests which contribute towards my wholeness.

✔ I am becoming less and less dependent on work for my self-esteem and self-worth.

✔ Work is something I choose to do joyfully, but is only one part of my increasingly rich and varied life.

✔ I am recognising that I contribute more to my work when I am refreshed and enriched by other interests.

✔ I am honouring the unique contribution I bring to life with every new interest I embrace.

✍ Your action list from this chapter

Write down at least six things that you intend to do now – ie, today not tomorrow – based on what you have learned in this chapter.

1

2

3

4

5

6

CHAPTER NINE

Working at 'Being'

"The wise soul without great doings achieves greatness."
Lao Tzu, *The Tao Te Ching*

A few years ago I was invited on a press trip to visit the Copenhagen head offices of a company whose products I had written about a number of times. It was a small group, comprising myself, three other freelance journalists and the then editor of *Human Resources* magazine, Godfrey Golzen. The trip was an enjoyable mix of sightseeing, discussing the company's products and debating various issues concerning the new world of work. On our way to Copenhagen airport to catch the flight back to London, I found myself sitting next to Godfrey, whom I hadn't really got to know during the visit. Because we now felt off duty after a stimulating but mentally draining couple of days, everyone was chatting generally rather than getting bogged down discussing work. Part of our discussion involved my telling Godfrey about the Open University psychology degree I was taking at the time. As is so often the case, because we were so engrossed in our conversation, the journey to the airport seemed to take no time at all, we said our goodbyes and took our seats in different parts of the plane.

Godfrey and I exchanged cards along with everyone else, but not once did I think of pitching an idea to him or trying to secure future commissions. I've seen journalists do this in the past and felt sorry for the editor being cornered, who was looking for nothing more demanding than a light-hearted chat in a social context. Our chat remained on a very friendly, personal level and not as a freelancer trying to impress an editor. Several months later I got a call from his deputy editor, who said they were looking for a journalist to write an article on psychometric testing and Godfrey had suggested me. I now produce a regular, monthly column for them on new and slightly off-the-wall HR initiatives.

The point being made here is that I got that work simply through being myself. I enjoyed talking to this man because he was interesting and interested, not because of what he did for a living and how this might benefit me in the future. I have learned through experience that when I stop trying so hard to make things happen they miraculously do anyway. And this from a recovering control junkie! From painful experience I realised I could never orchestrate two people talking about a specific need and having my name come up in conversation as the ideal person to fulfil it. Nor could I engineer the number of chance meetings that have taken place in my life, resulting in projects I have always wanted to do but never knew who to contact to get started.

One of the paradoxes of life is that taking action – or 'becoming' – based on these inner messages needs to be balanced with surrendering to the Universe. One example of this is going out socially but not being so desperate to find a new relationship that you put every potential suitor off. When you aren't looking or trying so hard is usually the time when love comes knocking on your door. The same is true of your work. Don't be fooled by thinking you have to spend all your time scanning job advertisements, improving your résumé and giving earache to everyone you meet about how you are looking for the job of your dreams. Life responds to a much subtler, internal approach.

~ Just be ~

Being can be so much more powerful than doing, yet is one of the hardest things for we human beings to accept. That's probably because almost from the day we are born we are socialised into believing we have to control life otherwise we won't get what we want. I have watched people try so hard to achieve something and become angry and frustrated when it hasn't happened. Perhaps if they'd stopped trying so hard to live in the future and enjoyed the present more, they would either have achieved their objective effortlessly or realised it wasn't really what was important after all.

In many respects the advice in this book requires a rebirth;

learning to embrace different attitudes and behaviours, to view life from a new, more spiritual perspective involves the same kind of pain and the same level of courage as our original births.

Nowhere have I come across a story more profoundly illustrative of this challenge than in Barbara de Angelis's book *Real Moments*. 'The woman who tried to climb the lake' is a most apt tale for anyone who truly wishes to work from the heart. In it a woman, who had spent her whole life climbing a mountain and had perfected all the skills needed to do this successfully, was suddenly confronted with a lake. Being a climber all her life, and having never seen a lake before, she thought that to cross the water she could simply use the same techniques she had used to master the mountain. She soon discovered that her efforts were not just useless but exhausting, but didn't know what to do until she noticed someone else floating by.

Similarly, many of us have spent so long 'doing' that we are unaccustomed to, and therefore struggle with, the concept of surrendering. Yet there gets to be a point in life when, to get where you need to go, it's more appropriate to 'float' than to 'climb'.

"The snow goose need not bathe to make itself white.
Neither need you do anything
but be yourself."
Lao Tzu

~ Find the Passion ~

Working from the heart is about contribution, love, self-expression, growth and learning, fulfilment, a sense of accomplishment. It's also about passion, a word we associate with intense feelings and arousing emotions, yet which comes from the Latin meaning 'to suffer or submit'. Passion is what keeps ballet dancers at the bars when their toes are bleeding and their tendons are stretched and aching. It's what ensures sports people are out on the track and field pushing them-selves that little bit harder, whether it's warm and sunny or freezing cold. Passion in the context of work is one of our greatest teachers because it demonstrates what it is we are pre-pared to suffer for and what we are not. When you are pas-sionate about what you do for a living every part of that work becomes a devotion, something you do with love and a feel-ing of service to others, even thought it sometimes involves mundane tasks, inconvenience, hard work and little external appreciation. In work, as in all other aspects of life, passion-ate people are successful. The irony is that it is the passion rather than the success which means the most to them.

The enduring vision that sustains me at times when my work is particularly challenging, frustrating or tedious is of metal being tempered in a furnace. Imagine a piece of gold ore which, in its natural state, isn't particularly attractive or cov-etable. Then imagine it being placed in the fire and beaten and worked on until it becomes the most exquisite piece of filigree. That's how life is for most of us: life burns us and beats us and wears us down. But if we have faith that one day we will be internally beautified by the wisdom, love and insight we have gained through these experiences – and that our lives have pur-pose and meaning – then we can bear anything in the process.

As Martine's story (page 113) illustrated, submitting to your calling doesn't mean life suddenly becomes easy or without its challenges; quite the contrary. Frequently it is even more chal-lenging, but, like a spiritual warrior akin to the heroes of Greek legend, you fulfil your destiny because you know that the ultimate prize is waiting for you at the end. That gift in human terms is the knowledge that you have touched people's lives, perhaps have inspired them with the courage and deter-mination to follow their own paths as you have yours, and have therefore made a difference. You have retrieved your soul.

"To be on a quest is nothing more or less than to become an asker of questions."
Sam Keen

✍ Exercise: Modelling others

Years ago, young people were apprenticed to older, experienced individuals, not just to learn technical skills, but also the attitudes and behaviours that went hand in hand with being an artisan. You can benefit from this approach by seeking out three or four individuals who love their work and talking to them about it. You could ask them:

● What is important to them and why?
● What meaning and purpose do they get from their work?
● What emotions come into play when they practise their vocation?
● How did they know it was their vocation in the first place?
● What challenges did they face to get where they are today?
● How do they cope when things get tough?
● Why do they do what they do?

However, never forget that in the process of being you are also becoming and that your vocation may also change with time. When you know yourself you accept that life is constantly about change, you learn to trust your intuition and believe that it will guide you to whatever you need to do in order to fulfil your destiny. You will then find it easier to let go of past programming and willingly immerse yourself in new approaches. My work metamorphoses to reflect the changes that are continually going on within me, as yours undoubtedly will. I am an author and journalist today, but who knows what I will feel passionate about in five, ten or fifteen years' time? Once you experience what it's like to work from the heart you will know that what's important – the thing from which everything else stems – is what's going on inside you. Once you experience what it's like to work from the heart you will never regret it.

Finally, here is an exercise to help you formulate a vision for something that is both unpredictable and chaotic, yet imaginable and self-created: your future.

🖎 Exercise: Working from the Heart

I invite you to write me a letter, dated six months, a year, or maybe even two years from now; whatever time frame you feel most comfortable with. The first paragraph has been completed for you; all you have to do is write the rest, letting me know how you managed to achieve finding work that engages your heart as well as your head. Remember that although this letter is being written for the future it should be worded in the present tense.

Once you have completed it you should pin it up where you can see it every day and use it as a template to move into this new possibility. Then, maybe, in six months, one or two years' time you would like to post that letter to me (see the next page for the address) because your dream of working from the heart has come true.

                                     Future date
Dear Liz Simpson,
I want to let you know that I am enjoying working from the heart, having found work that fulfils and excites me, having teamed up with wonderful, supportive colleagues in an inspirational environment where my innate skills and talents are being used to the full. I really love my work and want to tell you how it all came about: . . .

                                   Yours sincerely,
                                   (Your signature)

In their book *Megatrends 2000* authors John Naisbitt and Patricia Aburdence outline ten trends that we will experience in the next millennium. Aside from ones like 'the decade of women in leadership', 'religious revival' and 'the booming global economy', is 'the triumph of the individual'. I sincerely hope your life becomes increasingly triumphant, not least of which is your success in finding work that you love to do: working from the heart.

HeartWork™

The mission of HeartWork™ is to help change the way people and organisations view work, encouraging them to co-create a culture in which each individual feels able to bring his or her heart and soul, as well as mind and body, to the workplace. In so doing HeartWork™ hopes to positively affect the way we do business together – individually and corporately – as well as to improve the impact organisations have on the environment, and the advice offered to young people on marrying their dreams to their career aspirations.

HeartWork™ offers workshops and seminars, audio tapes and other material which has been developed into a modular programme based on the chapters in this book for use by companies, individuals and educational establishments.

In addition to being available as a key-note speaker and workshop facilitator, Liz Simpson – in conjunction with a chartered occupational psychologist – has devised a series of vocational assessment questionnaires. These checklists help build on the insights gained from this book and will direct you to the type of work that most aptly suits your values, interests, passion and abilities.

HeartWork™
PO Box 141
Sevenoaks, Kent,
TN15 0ZU, UK

Telephone: 07000 782899
Visit our website at: http://www.HeartWork.com/
And e-mail us at: heartwork@dial.pipex.com

Further Reading

Alder, Dr Harry, *Think Like a Leader*, Piatkus, 1995

Baldock, Robert, *Destination Z: The History of the Future*, John Wiley & Sons, 1999

Barrett, Richard, *A Guide to Liberating Your Soul*, Fulfilling Books, 1995

Black, Jack, *Mindstore*, Thorsons, 1994

Boyett, Joseph, and Boyett, Jimmie, *The Guru Guide: The Best Ideas of the Top Management Thinkers*, John Wiley & Sons, 1998

Breathnach, Sarah Ban, *Simple Abundance: A Daybook of Comfort and Joy*, Bantam Press, 1996

Boldt, Laurence G, *How to Find the Work You Love*, Penguin Arkana, 1996

Breaux, Charles, *The Way of Karma*, Samuel Weiser Inc, 1993

Bridges, William, *Job Shift: How to prosper in a workplace without jobs*, Nicholas Brealey Publishing, 1996

Brown, Dr Joy, *The Nine Fantasies That Will Ruin Your Life & the Eight Realities That Will Save It*, Crown Publishers NY, 1998

Canfield, Jack, and Miller, Jacquelin, *Heart at Work*, McGraw-Hill, 1998

Canfield, Jack, et al, *Chicken Soup for the Soul at Work*, Health Communications Inc, 1996

Childre, Doc Lew, *Freeze Frame*, Planetary Publications, 1994

Chopra, Deepak, *The Seven Spiritual Laws of Success*, Amber-Allen Publishing & New World Library, 1994

Chopra, Deepak, *Creating Affluence: The A to Z Steps to a Richer Life*, Amber-Allen Publishing & New World Library, 1993

Choquette, Sonia, *Your Heart's Desire*, Piatkus Books, 1997

Conner, Daryl R, *Leading At the Edge of Chaos*, John Wiley & Sons, 1998

Cooper, Cary, and Sutherland, Valerie, *30 Minutes to Deal with Difficult People*, Kogan Page, 1997

Cooper, Cary, and Jackson, Susan E, *Creating Tomorrow's Organisations: a handbook for future research in organisational behaviour*, John Wiley & Sons, 1997

Cousins, Norman, *The Anatomy of an Illness*, Bantam Books, 1981

Covey, Stephen, *Seven Habits of Highly Effective People: Powerful Lessons in Personal Change*, Simon & Schuster, 1992

Czikszentmihalyi, M, *Flow: The Psychology of Happiness*, Rider 1992

Czikszentmihalyi, M, *Creativity: Flow and the Psychology of Discovery and Invention*, Harper Perennial, 1997

De Angelis, B, *Real Moments*, Dell Publishing, 1994

Edwards, Gill, *Living Magically*, Piatkus Books, 1991

Farwagi, Peta Lyn, *The Life Balance Programme*, Orion Business Books, 1998

Frankl, Viktor E, *Man's Search for Meaning*, Washington Square Press, 1985

Hayward, Susan, *A Guide for the Advanced Soul*, In-Tune Books, 1984

Hemsath, Dave, and Yerkes, Leslie, *301 Ways to Have Fun at Work*, Berrett-Koehler Publishers, Inc, 1997

Holden, Robert, *Happiness Now!*, Hodder & Stoughton, 1998

Jeffers, Susan, *Feel the Fear and Do It Anyway*, Arrow 1991

Jeffers, Susan, *Feel the Fear ... and Beyond*, Rider, 1998

Jeffers, Susan, *End the Struggle and Dance with Life*, Hodder & Stoughton, 1996

Kingma, Daphne Rose, *Finding True Love*, Conan Press, 1996

Kushner, Harold S, *When Bad Things Happen to Good People*, Avon Books, 1981

Law, Andy, *Open Minds*, Orion Business Books, 1998

Leider, Richard, *The Power of Purpose: Creating meaning in your life and work*, Berrett-Koehler, 1997

Naisbitt, John, and Aburdence, Patricia, *Megatrends 2000*, Avon Books, 1990

Pearsall, Paul, PhD, *The Heart's Code*, Broadway Books, 1998

Redfield, James, *The Celestine Prophecy*, Bantam Books, 1994

Scott Peck, M, *The Different Drum*, Touchstone Books, 1998

Scott Peck, M, *The Road Less Travelled*, Arrow 1990

Secretan, Lance H K, *Reclaiming Higher Ground: Creating organisations that inspire the soul*, Macmillan Canada, 1996

Stemman, Roy, *Reincarnation*, Piatkus, 1997

Taylor, Jim, and Wacker, Watts, *The 500 Year Delta*, Capstone, 1997

Terkel, Studs, *Working: People talk about what they do all day and how they feel about what they do*, New Press, 1997

Thomson, Kevin, *Emotional Capital*, Capstone, 1998

Weatherall, M (Ed), *Identities, Groups and Social Issues*, SAGE publications in association with The Open University, 1996

Weinstein, Matt, *Managing to Have Fun*, Fireside, 1996

Whiteside, Patrick, *The Little Book of Happiness*, Rider, 1998

Wilks, Frances, *Intelligent Emotion*, William Heinemann, 1998

Williamson, Marianne, *A Return to Love: Reflections on the Principles of a Course in Miracles*, HarperCollins, 1996

Wilson, Paul, *Calm at Work*, Penguin, 1997

Wilson Schaef, Anne, *Meditations for Women Who Do Too Much*, Harper, San Francisco, 1992

Index

Aburdene, Patricia 185
accountancy 41–2
Achaan Chah Subato 52
action
  being yourself 180–1
  lists 69, 94, 115, 133, 167, 179
  taking 65, 80, 176
Adams, Scott 153
addictions 52, 170
affection 104
affirmations 67–9, 94, 115, 133, 146, 167, 179
Air Miles 34–5, 138
Alder, Dr Harry 89
Allied Domecq 136–7
alternative therapies 152
ambiguity 77, 79, 80, 93, 94
Angelis, Barbara de 182
Apollinaire, Guillaume 70
assumptions 78–9, 80, 94, 95–6
attitude
  to life 25–6, 49, 65, 182
  to relationships 148–9, 155–9
  to work
    balance 168
    cultural differences 24–5
    fun 134
    negative 13–14, 26–7
    passion 34–5, 41–2
authentic self 51–2, 65–6, 97, 106
auto-suggestion 67–8

balance 29–30, 75, 89, 104, 168–79
Barrett, Richard 145
behaviour patterns 65, 120–3, 182
being yourself 180–5
Bennett, Arnold 126
Black, Jack 17
Borge, Victor 143
brain 39–40, 67, 81
brand identity 83–6, 101, 102, 109–10
Breathnach, Sarah Ban 9, 77, 125
British Airways 34–5, 138, 166–7
Brontë, Emily 20
Brown, Dr Joy 127
Buddhism 7–8
busyness 52, 176

call-centres 34
career see work
Careerlink 166–7
challenges 23, 41, 52, 93, 106
change
  embracing 70–6, 184
  handling 76–7
  instigating 16, 19, 65, 114, 127–8
Chesterton, G K 145
children, job ideas 9, 30–2, 114
choice
  being what you choose 42–3
  goals 174–5
  of job 7–14, 22, 29, 31–2, 99–107
  and responsibility 49–50
  view of life 86
Chopra, Deepak 80, 116, 124, 125
Coelho, Paulo 132
coincidences 112–13
communication 66, 160–7, 174
companies
  flexible approach 82
  fun 134, 136–7
  scenario planning 90
  values 107–8
compliments 56, 143
conflict 147–8, 156–7, 165
Confucius 7, 33
consciousness 40, 67
control 25–6, 86, 122, 123–4
Cooper, Prof Cary 35, 169
core values 83–6, 101, 111, 123
Coue, Emil 67
Cousins, Norman 135
Covey, Stephen 66, 174
creativity 72–3, 135–6, 140, 146, 172
Csikszentmihalyi, Mihaly 62, 63
cultural attitudes 24, 111

Davies, Rowena 166
depression 51
detachment 79–81, 113
Dostoevsky, F M 155
dreams 31–2, 52, 174
Dunne, Dr Brenda 81
Dyer, Wayne 151

ego 46, 48, 49, 117, 150
Emmott, Mike 172
emotional capital 13, 38
emotions 147–8
employability 90, 94, 169
employees
  new 142, 143
  rewards 138, 139, 140–1, 142
  valuable asset 38
employment *see* work
empowerment 34–5, 66, 79
energy 23, 39–40, 124, 150–3
enlightenment 145, 149
enthusiasm 144, 165
exercises
  be your own best friend 55, 66–7
  brand identity 83–6, 109–10
  breaking behaviour patterns 121
  challenging assumptions 78–9
  changing your internal dialogue 92
  cost of work 132
  creating the future You 58–9
  financial planning 129–31
  give to receive 56
  handling change 76–7
  Heartwork Plan 101–2, 109–10
  life experiences 60–1
  modelling others 184
  perceptual positions 156–7
  power of nine 171–3
  seeing yourself 154, 158–9
  self-acceptance 57–8
  what is important to you? 18
  working from the heart 185
experience 9, 60–1, 105
expertise 103, 104

failure 115, 118
family
  importance 18, 103, 104, 169–71
  support 93
fears
  facing 64, 94, 132, 169
  overcoming 118–23
Ferguson, Marilyn 30
flexibility
  change 72, 94
  work 18, 29
flow experiences 62–3, 105
Ford, Henry 151
Frankl, Viktor 49, 51, 91, 97, 148
freelance work 11, 28
fulfilment, personal 14, 23, 105, 111,
  127–8
fun 132, 134–46

future
  Heartwork Plan 102, 103–5, 111–12
  planning 90–1, 93, 94, 123, 175

Gibran, Kahlil 43
giving
  to others 56, 125, 126, 133, 144
  to yourself 55, 56
goals
  achieving 119–20
  Heartwork Plan 103–5, 108, 113
  personal 16–17, 18, 63, 159
  SMART acronym 172–3
  trade-offs 174–5
Goethe, J W von 19
gratitude 56, 143, 144, 165
Gunther, Max 62
gut instincts 47, 51, 52, 62, 112–13

happiness
  at work 14, 23, 139
  Life Line 60–2
  riches 127, 129
  self-esteem 46
  ten steps to 143–5
head 37, 39–40, 67
health 14, 39–40, 52, 135
heart 37–40
Heartwork Plan 100, 101–15, 186
Higher Self 102, 105–8
Hill, Napoleon 125
Hirschberg, Robin 100
Hochman, Larry 34
Holden, Robert 143
home, working from 36
honesty 34, 47, 57, 120, 135, 165
housewives 87

identity 20–1, 46, 83–6, 101
impulsiveness 76
independence 103, 104
inner self 32, 51–2, 65–6, 97, 106

Jahn, Dr Robert G 81
Jeffers, Susan 58, 81
job satisfaction 20, 37, 99
job security 18, 27, 33, 35, 89
Jung, Carl Gustav 46, 57

Keen, Sam 183
Kingma, Daphne Rose 111

language, changing 92, 94
Lao Tzu 27, 49, 180, 182
laughter 135, 143, 146

leadership 103, 104, 166
Lee, Deborah 163
Leider, Richard 109–10
leisure activities 89
life
  analysing 65
  attitude to 25–6, 49, 65, 182
  as classroom 51, 148
  experiences 60–1
  positive approach 62
  purpose 23, 52, 110, 148
Life Line 60–1, 65, 76, 101, 105
losses, cutting 62, 122
loving yourself 55, 56, 64
luck 62, 122

Maeterlinck, Maurice 44
Marx, Karl 26
masking self 46–7, 52, 65–6, 97, 169
McKinsey & Co. 26
meditation 54, 145
memories 40, 60–1
mental problems 44–5, 51
mid-life crisis 15, 52, 53, 116
Midler, Bette 63
mission 98–9, 114
money
  cost of work 132
  earning 23
  financial planning 129–31
  financial security 20, 89, 122–3, 170
  importance 18, 103, 104, 116–23
  meaning 123–8
  saving 125–6, 128, 129, 130
  working with 41–2
motivation 22, 107, 111, 122, 166,
  172–3

Nadler, David 173
Naisbitt, John 185
needs
  order of importance 18, 52–3, 101,
    106–7
  of others 98–9, 125
  self-sacrifice 45, 46
  sine qua non 111
networking 62, 65, 80
Neuro Linguistic Programming 156
Nicholson McBride 18, 74, 103, 158
Nietzsche, F W 96

obsessive working 51, 168–70
opportunities 18, 75, 94, 109
Ortega y Gasset, Jose 73
out-of-the-box thinking 17, 78, 86, 95

pampering yourself 66–7
parental influence 30–1, 41, 44, 64,
  114
part-time working 35
passion
  finding 182–5
  flow experiences 62–3, 105
  in life 108
  in work 10–14, 22, 34–5, 98
Pearsall, Dr Paul 39, 40
pensioners 36–7
perceptual positions 156–7
perfect job 22–4, 64–7
Perls, Fritz 64
personal signatures 99, 110
personality 14, 23, 46, 57–9, 155
pessimism, nurturing 62
Peterman, John 115
Peters, Tom 37
Plato 134
pleasing yourself 66–7
pleasure 104, 105, 132, 133, 134–46
possessions 18, 117, 123, 125–6, 127
preconceptions 66, 77, 80, 94
prejudices 66
present, enjoying 144, 151
presenteeism 89, 169
prestige 103, 104, 118
problems 23, 41, 52, 89, 106
prosperity consciousness 124–5

quantum physics 50, 150–1, 152

reasons for working 20–2, 88
recruitment 33, 34
Redfield, James 152
redundancy, dealing with 87–91
reincarnation 50–1, 149–50
relationships
  attitude to 148–9, 155–9
  changes 76
  communication 160–7
  difficulties 20, 51, 89
  perception by others 158–9
  perception of others 156–7
  perception of self 154–5
  priorities 143
  working 147–67
religion 14, 25, 26, 50
responsibility 49–50, 64, 135, 164
retraining 45
risk taking 62, 75, 119–23
Roddick, Anita 9, 11
role models 65, 111, 184
routine tasks 63

Saint-Exupéry, Antoine de 38
St-James, Elaine 125
scenario planning 90–1, 93, 123, 175
Secretan, Lance H K 116, 138
self-acceptance 57–8, 64
self-deception 44–5
self-esteem 20, 45, 46–8, 51, 122, 164
self-expression 21, 32–3
self-realisation 104, 105
self-respect 90
self-sacrifice 45
self-understanding 15, 24, 40, 49, 110
Sendak, Maurice 176
serendipity 99–100, 112, 122, 181
service to others 63, 98–9, 103, 104,
   110, 166
short-term contracts 28, 29, 36
sickness absence 14, 35, 40, 135
Simpson, Liz, early career 9–11
sine qua non 111–12, 163
skills
   developing 90
   interpersonal 148, 166
   matching to job 47–8, 68–9, 97–8
   outside work 87, 142
SMART acronym 172–3
Smith, Larry 110
social activities 18, 20, 137, 138, 140
soul 40, 50–1, 98, 117, 127, 149–50,
   183
spontaneity 75, 76
status 20, 89, 103, 118, 170
Stemmen, Roy 50
strengths and understrengths
   brand identity 109
   perception of others 158–9
   playing to 48
   self-acceptance 57
stress 13, 39, 51, 135
success 118–19
Sweeney, Anne 10
Szekely, Edmond Boreaux 19

team building 135–7, 139, 141, 160–1
Terkel, Studs 27
The 4 per centers 16–17
threats, Heartwork Plan 109
Tichy, Prof Noel M 54
Tigrett, Isaac 9, 11, 12
time, balancing 175–6
tiredness 45, 51
tithing 125
training 136–7
truth 120

uncertainty 80, 94
unemployment
   breaks from work 29–30
   dealing with 51, 87–91
   self-esteem 46
Unique Selling Point 110

values
   companies 107–8
   comparing 106–7
   conflict of 107–8
   core 83–6, 101, 111, 123
   money 123–4, 126–7, 133
   spiritual 145
   and work 98
visualisation 54, 90–1, 174–5, 175
vocational choice 7–14, 22, 31–2, 90,
   99–107, 184
Voltaire 26, 156
voluntary simplicity 125, 129, 131
voluntary work 88

weaknesses see strengths and
   understrengths
weekends 22, 23, 26
Weinstein, Matt 146
Whyte, David 13, 53
Wilks, Frances 108, 147
Williamson, Marianne 31, 119
Woodroffe, Simon 9, 11, 12, 137
work
   attitude to 24–5
   breaks from 29–30
   changing 161–3, 177–8
   changing patterns 25, 27–8, 35–7
   choosing 7–14, 22, 31–2, 99–107,
      184
   cost of 132
   fun 134 -46
   long-term prospects 24, 28
   matching skills to job 47–8, 68–9,
      97–8
   as mission 98–9
   reasons for 20–2
   relationships 147–67
   self-expression 32–3
workaholism 89, 168–9, 177
working environment 18, 111
working life 18, 36–7

Yale University 16–17
Yo!Sushi 137

Zander, Sir Benjamin 42, 77